CRV

Controlled Remote Viewing

Manuals, collected papers &
information to help you learn this
intuitive art.

Daz Smith

"QUIS CUSTODIET IPSOS CUSTODES?"

(Who watches the watchmen?)

2013 Daz Smith

ISBN-10:1482674181
ISBN-13: 978-1482674187

DEDICATION

This is dedicated to the people who worked diligently and under great trials and tribulations over many years to create the amazing tool of Controlled Remote Viewing.

The original source - Ingo Swann, Hal Puthoff, Tom McNear, Paul H Smith & the many others named and nameless from inside SRI & the U.S. military Remote Viewing programs from 1972 to 1995, and beyond.

CONTENTS

ABOUT REMOTE VIEWING?

Remote viewing is a mental faculty that allows a person to sketch and give details about a target that is inaccessible to normal senses due to distance or time.

As practitioners we have to be honest from the start and inform all interested parties that no matter how much you are willing to pay to be trained in **any** methodology of Remote Viewing, be this the focus of this book or one of the many others on offer, there is no guarantee that training will make you a Remote Viewing Jedi.

Becoming a competent Remote Viewer does, ultimately, rely on a combination of components all contributing to the overall depth of the Remote Viewers' skills.

No matter what you may have read or heard online or in books, CRV as a form of psychic training was not intended and never was taught to people showing zero psychic ability. All the original participants in the military CRV training programme showed a natural psychic ability and they were sought out for the unit because of this 'natural ability'. CRV on its own will not make anyone more psychic or a better Remote Viewer. This applies to all the Remote Viewing methods on the market, no matter how much they cost.

To be a good Remote Viewer requires several ingredients: time and practice. Bruce Lee didn't get to be the best martial artist of his generation on raw talent alone, or practice alone. It was his dedication to the art, his talent and his practice over many, many years that allowed his to flourish - to expand - to realize his full potential.

To be good at being a Remote Viewer consist of several key ingredients:

1. Natural ability.
The more natural ability, the better the Remote Viewer. All the other ingredients 'help', but the core natural ability determines your overall proficiency. If you have never had an accurate psychic or intuitive experience before CRV training, then no amount of training will make you the best RV Jedi in the world, on its own. Natural ability is the baseline.

2. Dedication.
Learning CRV will take you years. There may never be an end to the things you learn and to where the road takes you. I have been working within CRV for

over fifteen years and every day, every project teaches me something new.

You need to have the right frame of mind when you embark on CRV training. You won't be an RV Jedi in weeks, months or maybe even years. It's a long journey, but also a very fruitful journey.

3. Practice.

I, like so many others, have found that reinforcement through practice does improve my skills. Again, like 'dedication' this is part of the process that takes years. Every single practice session is a learning experience, and believe me you learn more from the misses than from the hits, so do not be discouraged - ALL Remote Viewers (at times) miss the target.

4. Method.

Now this is where we get controversial. There are many knowledgeable people within Remote Viewing who do claim that there is no proof that a method like CRV improves RV performance. I disagree and the paper evidence from the 91,000 plus pages of released CIA Star Gate files supports what I believe and know from actual experience. Any method, mixed with dedication, natural ability, and practice will help the natural ability flourish. A Remote Viewing method alone will not teach you how to become psychic, but it can clarify and build upon your existing natural ability and improve it.

Be aware, if any of these (above) components are missing from the mix, then the recipe for the perfect RV Jedi does not come together as it should. CRV or ANY Remote Viewing method is not a short cut.

WHAT IS CRV?

Controlled Remote Viewing (CRV) is an art form. Its nearest comparison I can find is a mental martial art. CRV's methodology; its use of drills and repetition, that embed a reflexive action and structure into the viewer, is a work of genius from its creator - Ingo Swann and Hal Puthoff, the founders of CRV, who actively worked on the development of CRV at SRI from 1976 to 1986.

Ingo and Hal analyzed every element of internal processing that Ingo and other psychics experienced when Remote Viewing. In doing so they created a method that 'helps' the intuitive take control of what had always been a spontaneous mechanism. As well as giving the intuitive control, CRV provides tools to lessen the hindrance of 'noise' created as the ego tries desperately to please and to recognize the incoming data, by filling-in the gaps with guesses.

Now, you'll notice I said lessen and not stop. There will always be some kind of 'noise' in the process. Remote viewing is NOT 100% accurate 100% of the time. The very best Remote Viewers still have 'noise' within their work. Until we fully know the mechanisms behind PSI and the Remote Viewing process, all attempts to stop the 'noise' have only helped lessen it.

The CRV method created by Ingo is a six stage process. Each stage builds on the one before, opening an ever wider aperture to the target. The entire CRV process is a creative process - it's an artistic expression from start to finish. It's why the Ideogram works so ingeniously. It's also why sketches within CRV capture so much data with a few, sharp sketchy lines. The same place from which inspiration, ideas, and artistic flow is the same place as Remote viewing data flows - it's all the same thing.

CRV is expression of a remote target through an ideogram, then sketches of the target, then more detailed sketches, later still maybe even a sculpture (model) of the target - it's art and creativity hidden within a structured environment to report data in a way that most people feel comfortable with.

In simple terms, CRV starts with a doodle, then it moves to basic sketches, then more detailed sketches, then models and sculptures. All this within a few rules and six small incremental stages.

THE MANUALS & PAPERS

The first paper presented in this compilation is from the CIA Star Gate archives. Authored by Ingo Swann, the document is titled: 'Co-ordinate Remote Viewing (CRV) Technology 1981-1983, Three Year Project'. It is a rare insight into Ingo's development of CRV training, and its results from this early developmental period.

I would like to state at this point that Ingo Swann never endorsed nor promoted Any CRV training services or materials for others to use in any course or training scenario. There are no such official affiliations.

After this we present two CRV manuals. The first is by Ingo Swann's top CRV student, Tom McNear, the only person trained in all CRV stages by Ingo Swann. This is titled: 'Coordinate Remote Viewing Stages I-VI and Beyond' - 1985.'[3]

The second, a later manual, first put online in 1998 by PJ Gaenir, was created by Paul H. Smith and others from the military Controlled Remote Viewing unit , titled: 'The DIA CRV Manual – 1986'[6].

Each version has its own distinct style and its own merits - which is why we have included both.

I would like to make it clear that this compilation is not the ideal way to learn Remote Viewing or the method of Controlled Remote Viewing (CRV). The best way would be with a competent teacher on a close one-to-one basis or in a small class. This compilation of papers and manuals are a reference guide for people wanting to learn CRV to be best used with class notes, training and lots and lots of practice. Using the manuals alone, though not impossible, is not recommended.

CO-ORDINATE REMOTE VIEWING (CRV) TECHNOLOGY - 1981-1983

THREE-YEAR PROJECT

Prepared for:
Dr. H. E. Puthoff
Radio Physics Laboratory
SRI International
CLASSIFIED BY: DT-5A

Ingo Swann (consultant)
30 August 1983

GENERAL DESCRIPTION

In 1981, a three-year training program concerning potentials in CRV was established. I was mandated, through consulting contracts, to organize the work and tutor the selected personnel and technical elements of this program. The specific sponsors and work designs for this program may be found in other documents. The three-year program is now at an end. What follows constitutes a summary report of the work undertaken, the results obtained, and certain projections for future work if a renewed effort is mandated.

WHAT WAS THE GOAL?

The overall goal of the CRV training program was to create, out of the features of CRV previously discovered, a training program through which the elements of successful coordinate remote viewing would be transferred to client preselected trainees. Any success in achieving this, implied answers to two items which were of paramount interest at the beginning of the three-year program:

(1) That the specific elements of the CRV methodology were not unique to their inventor.

(2) That these elements, given instructional body, could be transferred into the client community.

TYPES OF TRAINEES ENGAGED

During the three-year program, Viewer A acted as the general R&D source person, applied to himself as a test what was discovered, and what was organized as a nucleus training course.

Subsequent to this, the first group of viewer trainees

(Viewers B, C, and D) embarked on training. This first group had the distinction of being, prior to entering upon the training course, composed of persons who had had psi experience and had acted as experimental subjects in several other kinds of parapsychological experiments.

Subsequent to the first group, a second group (Viewers E, F, G, H, I) was enrolled as a further test of the methodologies evolved by Viewer A.

This second group was composed of professional people, each of whom had achieved success in their various fields of interest, but none of which had acted before as an overt psychic-type of person in parapsychological experiments.

After positive results of the second group were well in hand, one of the clients was invited to send preselected trainees (Viewers J and K).

Subsequent to this, another client sent one preselected trainee (Viewer 1) during the last half of the three-year period.

STAGES OF TRAINING

The training procedures have been broken down into several stages representing various elements of CRV phenomena. These stages both facilitate training, and actually follow the predictable course of increasing perception which builds itself by specific increments and
importance's. Stages 1 through 3 have been confirmed and delivered to trainees. Stage 4 and Stage 6 have been confirmed and are ready to be

delivered to trainees upon their completion of Stage 3. Stage 5 is understood, but has not yet been solidified into a training package.

Stages 1 through 3 appertain to large site features, which become increasingly refined as a result of command over the Stage 3 techniques.

Stage 4 involves perception of specific and often invisible site elements, a good portion of which may not be available to any other intelligence gathering techniques, save for actual penetration of the site.

Stage 5 will allow the viewer to "turn around" and begin to interrogate the signal line for specific subtle features of several kinds. *See Figure 1.*

Stage 6 allows for the construction of 3-dimensional models of the major site characteristics with increasing refinements in particulars.

THE STAGES

	SKILL GAINED	SIGNAL BROUGHT UNDER CONTROL
STAGE 1.	IDEOGRAMS AND IDEOGRAM PRODUCTION	SIGNALS THAT INDUCE/PRODUCE IDEOGRAMIC RESPONSES (GESTALTS)
STAGE 2.	SENSATIONS EXPERIENCED FROM DISTANT SITE	SIGNALS PRODUCING TACTILE, SENSORY, DIMENSIONAL ESTIMATES, DIRECTIONAL FEELINGS, AND SO FORTH
STAGE 3.	MOTION AND MOBILITY (LIMITED) AT DISTANT SITE RESULTING IN PRIMARY ARTISTIC RENDERINGS	SIGNALS PRODUCING AESTHETIC RESPONSES IN VIEWER, SIMPLE SKETCHES AND "TRACKERS"
STAGE 4.	QUANTITATIVE AND QUALITATIVE ASSESSMENTS OF VARIOUS DISTANT SITE CHARACTERISTICS	SIGNALS (MANIFOLD) THAT INDUCE ANALYTICAL COMPREHENSIONS
STAGE 5.	METHODS OF INTERROGATING THE SIGNAL LINE	(STILL IN R&D)
STAGE 6.	CREATING 3-DIMENSIONAL MODELS	SIGNALS (CONSOLIDATED) THAT YIELD SIMPLE REPLICAS OF DISTANT SITE FEATURES
STAGE 7.	SONICS (STILL IN R&D)	SIGNALS THAT INDUCE VERBAL CONTENT
STAGE 8.	HUMAN TO HUMAN INTERFACES (R&D, 1984/1985)	SIGNALS THAT IMPLY HUMAN PSYCHIC EMPATHY AND INDUCE/PRODUCE IDEOGRAMIC RESPONSES (GESTALTS)

FIGURE 1 THE STAGES

WHAT HAS BEEN ACHIEVED

A. Training Has Been Achieved

Relevant to Stages 1 through 3, all trainees who embarked on the training course responded exceedingly well to the training procedures. The second group worked quite slowly due to other personal commitments and scheduling.

Among the first sponsor-selected trainees, Trainee K is nearing completion of Stage 3; Trainee J has temporarily left the course due to serious health problems. The second sponsor-selected candidate only entered the program in 1983, but is progressing satisfactorily.

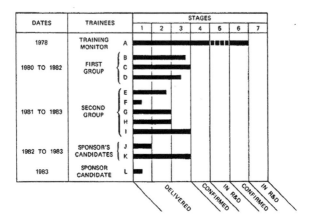

FIGURE 2 THREE-YEAR PROGRAM CRV
TRAINEES/ACCOMPLISHMENTS

B. The Phenomena Trained are not Unique to, Gifted, Psychics.

The overall context of the training course and the success of the given trainees has established that the basic psi-perceptual phenomena are not unique to "gifted" psychics and that given adequate understanding of them and carefully constructed training and practical exercises, selected candidates can take command of the phenomena encountered.

C. A New Understanding Has Been Achieved

With the comprehensions we now have in hand, it is clear that the psychical perceptual task is of a delicacy and complexity that goes far beyond any given understanding of it entertained in parapsychology in general. This places us in a status that obliges us to bear two things constantly in mind:

(1) So-called standard approaches normally utilized in parapsychology are predictably limited.

(2) The most fruitful future work probably will be built upon the knowledge and understanding of the phenomena taken control of during the three year project.

WHERE ARE WE GOING

A. Enlargement of the Training Pool

In terms of future work, it is feasible and desirable to further enlarge the training pool.

B. Delivery of Stage 4

It is important that Stage 4, confirmed, packaged and ready to be delivered, be tutored to those who have completed Stage 3. Locating and stabilizing the elements of Stage 4 was quite difficult and it was in R&D for nearly two years. It involves a significant "jump" from configurational data decoded out of Stages 1 through 3, into subtle data that bear significant intelligence potential. Once Stage 4 was stabilized and self trained by Viewer A, a significant incremental difference immediately manifested in classified site viewings as is shown in Figure 2 below. Stage 4 was applied by Viewer A to certain sites after Stage 4 had been isolated and confirmed. On a rating of intelligence value of 0 to 3, the pre-Stage 4 sites averaged 1.21 while those that incorporated Stage 4 techniques averaged 2.75. See figure 3 below.

PRE-STAGE 4			STAGE 4		
DIA Eval	Site #	Date	DIA Eval	Site #	Date
1	J.S. #1	12 Feb 80	2+	J.S. #39	8 Feb 83
1	J.S. #3	13 Feb 80	3	J.S. #40	10 Feb 83
1+	J.S. #5	3 Mar 80	3	J.S. #41	11 Feb 83
2	J.S. #8	1 Jul 80	2+	J.S. #42	11 Feb 83
2	J.S. #12	2 Apr 81	2.75 Average		
Abort	J.S. #13	3 Apr 81			
2	J.S. #14	7 Apr 81			
0	J.S. #15	8 Apr 81			
0	J.S. #16	8 Apr 81			
3	J.S. #17	9 Apr 81			
2+	J.S. #20	8 Jun 81			
1	J.S. #21	6 Aug 81			
1	J.S. #29	14 Dec 81			
0+	J.S. #30	14 Dec 81			
2-	J.S. #31	14 Dec 81			
No eval	J.S. #33	7 Jan 82			
1	J.S. #34	1 Mar 82			
0+	J.S. #35	4 Nov 82			
1	J.S. #36	5 Nov 82			
1+	J.S. #37	15 Nov 82			
0	J.S. #38	21 Jan 83			
1.21 Average					

FIGURE 3 PRE- AND POST-STAGE 4
ACHIEVEMENTS AVERAGED

C. An R&D Potential for "SEARCH" Has Come Into View

In terms of future work, the problem of "SEARCH" should achieve a platform of understanding that has not hitherto been available under standard parapsychological approaches. These breakthroughs are expected to arrive through the context of Stage 5 (interrogation of the signal line). Although Stage 5 is still in R&D as concerns the packaging and delivery of it, there are sufficient indicators already present to indicate that the problem of search will be addressed, at least in some important understandings, through continued mapping of it.

It must be noted carefully, and based upon our ten years of experience now, that any resolution to the "SEARCH" problem probably will only be achieved if we arrive at some understanding of how it is that the signal line might be profitably interrogated. The danger will be to proceed with ad hoc experiments which, even if marginally successful, might not yield any basic understandings leading ultimately to controlled interrogation procedures.

The achievement of finding a significant aperture through which the signal line can be interrogated without also arousing volumes of "noise" is therefore an important prerequisite for the "SEARCH" problem.

D. The Electromagnetic Connection

During the overall course of the R&D and training, sufficient phenomena have surfaced that indicate a direct connection of viewer performance with certain geomagnetic conditions. The daily parameters of basic earth electromagnetic conditions therefore achieved some interest on our part. An "eye-ball" scan of these interrelationships clearly indicates an important, but hitherto unsuspected, interaction between viewing and success in correctly interpreting the signal line and electromagnetic conditions. We expect that this unsuspected relationship will bear itself out, and if so, establish in some form the first verifiable psielectromagnetic relationships. This in turn portends the arrival of understandings that concern countermeasures.

In the estimation of this consultant, bearing in mind the significances of the several steps forward that have come into view during the last work epoch, the biomagnetic/psi perceptual problem should probably be given highest and first priority. The fact that earth's geomagnetic field and human physiology and psychology are both influenced by and interact. with EMF has been established quite some time ago *(See Pressman, A.S., Electromagnetic Fields and Life, Plenum Press, New York (Prof. Pressman, Department of Biophysics, Moscow University, Moscow).)* Based upon experience, if the work should proceed under the "spontaneous result" philosophy or attitude, there will be a tendency to replicate more familiar approaches.

The EMF/consciousness/psi area is unfamiliar to most of us; yet, based upon our observations, there is an astonishing degree of correlation. It is strongly recommended that an organized interest in this special phenomena be given priority.

VII DISCUSSION

A. Background

In considering this report on Coordinate Remote Viewing (CRV) work, several important distinguishing features may be borne in mind.

An in-depth review of the history of formal psychical or paranormal research--covering some 100 years-- clearly reveals that no successful training methodologies have been located or evolved prior to the work undertaken at SRI, specifically in CRV. While certain epochs of psychical work in the past have extraordinary merit, these for the most part have had as their goal the establishing of credibility that the several psychical manifestations do exist. These manifestations have been contacted in a spontaneous form, and displays of their arrays always have been dependent upon the innate "giftedness" of subjects if they emerged or could be located. The spontaneous forms have not in a continuing form lent themselves very well to the scientific parameters designed to "capture" them. Because of this, the "field" or "state-of-the-art," as a whole, was forced to view the spontaneous arrays through, usually, statistical methods of evaluation and averaging.

The statistical approaches have sufficed to establish credibility for the existence of spontaneous paranormal aptitudes in given individuals or groups; by itself, however, it has not been sufficient or capable of extrapolating on the exact nature of aptitude-characteristics in any given and continuable psychical manifestation.

Furthermore, seeking to utilize statistical approaches to the problems before them, psychical researchers ultimately came to seek experiments that might better increase the statistical averages they sought. This overall approach led to a drastic proliferation of random experimentations that had as their goals more experimental design but often affiliated them less with actual psychical aptitudes. Throughout this history, the actual problem of psychical manifestations has been addressed only tangentially, if at all, prior to the present CRV work.

This problem consists of two equally important factors:

(1) What makes superior data, when it emerges, superior?

(2) What makes inferior data, when it emerges, inferior?

This dual problem is a problem for research (rather than random experimentation) into the different factors that govern the perceptual modes that underlay this extraordinary duality. In approaching this duality, the statistical averaging or evaluation of experiments of the superior into the inferior data is and has been of little avail in that it does not lead into intimate contact with the perceptual attributes involved.

The hallmark of the CRV R&D work-leading to training capabilities-has been to concentrate upon the exact nature of <u>both</u> superior and inferior arrays of data and to plumb into the exact nature of the perceptual attributes involved in each of them. It was assumed, at the outset, and correctly so, that superior data contained less or least false data among its overall contents, and that inferior data were data sets in which most of the content was false. Superior data, therefore, were data relatively free of false data, and it became easy to think of the overall problem as one of signal versus noise. The characteristics both of signal and noise had to be discovered and isolated, and it is the cumulative breakthroughs in this history that have led to constant progress in CRV R&D and, ultimately, to a training program based upon those breakthroughs so far discovered.

B. The Definition of Training

Prior to a training program being established, no specific set of methods or practices had been brought into existence that elevated psychical aptitudes or attributes above just merely attempting to encourage the emergence of spontaneous displays. It had been in the recent past, possible to give general orientation to individuals about the nature of psychical abilities, and thereafter leave it to themselves to attempt to evoke spontaneous psychical displays.

It is the definition of "training" that gives the CRV project a considerable difference from orientation and spontaneous displays of psychic aptitudes. "Training" implies a prefigured regime that will, if correctly applied, lead to predictable performance which, in turn, will yield superior results. Such a training program should be considered viable if, together with increasing discoveries, it continues to develop along lines of increasingly refined results and precision.

The R&D training project has well established that predictable performance can be trained; and its results correctly extrapolated into use oriented functions. Furthermore, the overall approach utilized in R&D continues to reveal increasingly refined capabilities which in turn, as of the close of the three-year project, imply pending entrance into some truly interesting areas of tactical concern.

C. Epochs of CRV R&D and Training

Exploration and development of Coordinate Remote Viewing (CRV) has gone through many phases: from random experimenting in 1974, ultimately to its substantive contents now isolated into a primary, but standardized, training course.

Based strictly upon the increasing success of trainees, it is anticipated that the CRV procedures will continue to increase in value as a practical applications tool. See Figure 4 below. It is nearly impossible to talk in detail of the complexity of the tasks of precision and

perceptual-control with, which the viewer-trainee is faced as he or she begins to try to achieve command over the signal line. The reality of the multiple tasks involved only become apparent to the trainees during the course of their training through each subsequent stage.

1. EXPLORATORY	1972 TO 1975
2. INTERVENING AREA	1974 TO 1976
3. PROBLEM OF SIGNAL vs NOISE	1976 TO 1978
4. FUNDAMENTAL PERCEPTUAL STUDIES	1977 TO 1979 AND CONTINUING
5. ISOLATION OF THE IDEOGRAM	1979
6. TRAINING/LEARNING	1980 — PRESENT AND CONTINUING
7. INTENSIVE ENHANCEMENT	1982 AND CONTINUING
8. PROJECTION OF OPERATIONAL READINESS	1983 AND CONTINUING

FIGURE 4 - EPOCHS OF COORDINATE
REMOTE VIEWING R&D

D. The Precision of CRV

R&D, aligned with training, have shown that "psychic" signals offer themselves up to interpretative consciousness through a predictable series of "signal impulses." This series starts with "greatest" meaning, and evolves into "specific" components.

This predictable process has easily yielding "stages" each of which, in training, can be specifically tutored.

It is important to establish, in the context of this first overall report on CRV training, that these tasks are of extraordinary delicacy and require precision control, as will be exhibited by the trainees upon completion of each stage of training. The psychological perspective that necessarily is required to surround this operation, should be seen as a new contribution to overall perceptual psi requirements. This psychological perspective should not be assumed to resemble any other forgoing idea of requirements in the area of general spontaneous psi displays.

E. The CRV Training Course is Carefully Designed

The most important task in creating the CRV training course was to come to grips with the subtle factors involved in accepting the fact that the self-generating creative faculties of the trainee would achieve prime importance.

The second task was to design an approach that might incorporate psychic functions on a strict and repetitive basis, and yet not drive these emerging functions into extinction.

The result has been the devising of a course of training that has produced satisfactory results in these very important areas. Analysis of learning patterns, display patterns that are recognizable in other disciplines of training in which a new performance-skill is gained through precision tutoring or coaching. See Figure 5

```
WHAT ARE WE ASKING THE TRAINEE TO DO?

   • TO CONTACT A DISTANT SITE BY MEANS OTHER THAN NORMAL
     SENSORY EXPERIENCE

   • TO ACHIEVE A COMPREHENSION THAT INFORMATION IS AVAILABLE
     THROUGH NONSENSORY CHANNELS

   • TO ACTIVATE PARTICIPATION IN THESE INFORMATION CHANNELS

   • TO ACTIVATE AND FORM NEW SKILLS TO DO SO

   • TO PUT THESE NEW SKILLS ON A CONTROLLABLE AND PREDICTABLE
     BASIS
```

FIGURE 5 THE CRV TRAINING TASK

F. How is Progress Judged?

It has transpired that the learning patterns of the CRV training do exhibit great similarities to other learning-patterned tasks in which a new skill involving consciousness interpretation vis a vis neuro-motor functioning is gained: (i.e., sports, musical performance, machinery driving, flying, navigating, etc.).

We therefore interpret that the psychical component of CRV is not solely one of intellectual mentation, but one in which mental-physical performance is achieved.

As with a number of fields, the elements of the performance of which respond to careful tutoring, we find, during the course of CRV training first a "spontaneous" performance closely related to the "first time" phenomenology. After that, as the trainee attempts to take over both on a cognitive level and on an unconscious habit-forming control of both physical and mental responses, we see a high elevation of "noise."

Shortly thereafter, as the varied elements of the tasks become organized within the intellectual-mental attributes of the trainee, we see a quick "consolidation" of the task aptitudes involved. At the end of this consolidating experience, the new skill or "plateau" emerges. See fig; 6 below.

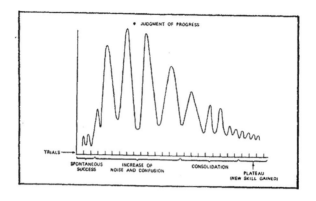

FIGURE 6 - CONSOLIDATION/PLATEAU PATTERN

During the course of training on each element, within the "stages," the viewer-trainee will predictably progress through this progress pattern. Therefore, the results of each trainee both can be monitored while the training progresses, and his overall pattern of response can be displayed through the graph plan found in Figure 6 above.

Actual graphs of selected viewers will be found in Annex A. The selected graphs are few to achieve optimum understanding; it should be borne in mind that all the viewers trained have responded with near similarity to each other.

G. CRV Training Course Methods and Protocols

The general elements of the CRV training course are presented below in Figures 7 through 9.

(a) The design and establishment of the CRV training course necessitated a great deal of research into methodologies of other fields. The most effective instructional procedures ultimately utilized are found in Figure 8 below.

(b) The CRV training course is comprised of a general design, whose elements are followed in each stage of the training. While each element is of importance in its place, the element pertaining to "reactive inhibition" achieves predominant placement. This has to do with understanding the phenomena associated with "overtraining" the result of which causes the trainee to exhibit negative effects of disinterest, etc., the ultimate result of which is a type of inhibition in producing the desired elements of the training. In other psi research experiments, this inhibition achieved notoriety under the terminology of "psi-missing." It is a simple psychological affect that can be guarded against. See Figure 9.

(c) The training course also includes several special features which are applicable to the psi task at hand in each stage. The feedback protocol was designed to reinforce the trainee's contact with the signal line but not to assist him with random cuing. The use of essays will exhibit the trainee's current understanding of each phenomena, and can be used to uncover areas of misunderstanding that the training monitor cannot spot in advance. See Figure 9.

- EFFECTIVE INSTRUCTIONAL PROCEDURES

    - *ACTIVE PARTICIPATION:* THE LEARNER IS ACTIVELY INTERACTING WITH THE CURRICULUM MATERIALS BY RESPONDING, PRACTICING, AND TESTING EACH STEP OF THE MATERIAL TO BE MASTERED.

    - *INFORMATION FEEDBACK:* THE LEARNER FINDS OUT WITH MINIMAL DELAY WHETHER THE RESPONSE IS CORRECT. IMMEDIATE FEEDBACK HAS BEEN SHOWN TO BE IMPORTANT IN A RANGE OF TASKS.

    - *INDIVIDUALIZATION OF INSTRUCTION:* THE LEARNER MOVES AHEAD AT HIS OR HER OWN RATE.

FIGURE 7 - INSTRUCTIONAL PROCEDURES

- GENERAL DESIGN OF CURRICULUM MATERIALS

    - THEORY

    - PRACTICAL EXERCISES AND DRILLS

    - INFORMATION FEEDBACK

        - SIGNAL LINE
        - COACHING ON CONTROL OF STRUCTURE

    - INDIVIDUALIZATION OF INSTRUCTION

    - REACTIVE INHIBITION

    - ENDING OF PRACTICAL SESSIONS

    - DAILY REPORTS

    - FINAL SURVEY

FIGURE 8 - GENERAL DESIGN

- SPECIAL FEATURES
  - FEEDBACK PROTOCOL
    - SILENCE, IF SOME STATEMENT IS WRONG
    - PROBABLY CORRECT (PC)
    - NEAR (N)
    - CAN'T FEEDBACK (CFB)
    - CORRECT (C)
    - SITE (S)
  - USE OF ESSAYS
  - CONSTANT OBSERVATION OF TRAINEES' ATTITUDES
  - CONSTANT SUPERVISION FOR POSSIBLE MISCOMPREHENSIONS OR MISUNDERSTANDINGS

FIGURE 9 - SPECIAL FEATURES

H. Summary of Increase in Yields

While there is, of course, yet a significant amount of work to be done, especially relative to training in the upper complex stages, the following generalized graph illustrates general increase of yields (1980-1983) in several categories of importance. See figure 10...

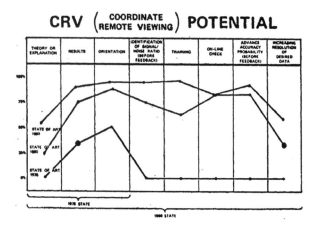

FIGURE 10
FIVE-YEAR INCREASE IN YIELDS (1978-1983)

Examples of Stage 1 progress in graph form

With reference to the consolidation/plateau pattern as shown in figure 6, each trainee proceeds to learn through four recognizable patterns of learning: spontaneous success, increase of noise as separate elements are dealt with separately, consolidation of the elements, and, finally, a new plateau of skill. In the following figure 11 and 12, the elements of two sponsor selected trainees J & K are shown, and these are compared with first group trainees B & C. It can be seen that the learning patterns are approximately the same, the end product being conscious control of the signal and a generating of an accurate and noiseless signal line.

As of the writing of this report, two trainees (I & K) are nearing completion of stage 3, An additional

30

report will be tendered concerning stage 3 upon their completion.

Stage 4 has been confirmed, packaged, and is awaiting delivery to training candidates who have successfully completed stage 3.

THE FIRST CRV MANUAL

In 1985 Thomas (Tom) M. McNear, Lieutenant Colonel, US Army (ret.) wrote the first CRV manual based on his training with Ingo Swann. Tom was the first military trained remote viewer trained by Ingo and was also the prototype for Ingo's new training method (CRV) and was hailed by Ingo as his best ever student. Tom was the only member Ingo Swann trained through Stage VI; he was the "proof of principle guinea pig." Tom's later sessions also began to evolve into Stage VII (phonetics), naming many sites by name via phonetics.

Paul H. Smith wrote: "Tom's results were not just impressive. Some could even be considered spectacular."

Of Toms CRV training Ingo wrote: "I believe it is appropriate here to comment overall on the character and nature of this particular trainee (TM). I recommend that we forward to the client our congratulations on this product of their selection methods, which are, apparently, excellent. In all instances, and even under certain project hardships, this trainee: exhibited what can only be rated as high and professional demeanor throughout. He was able to apply himself at all times with the utmost of intellectual accuracy to all the tasks and training drills that were encountered. lie was able to perform even all the tedious drills necessary, to maintain his performances within the standards that have been inbuilt into the training model, and, finally, to emerge at the ether end. of the training with new and consolidated aptitudes. while we do not, of course, yet have enormous numbers from ·which we might draw comparisons, it should be stated to the client that in the case of this trainee, he exhibited the least of difficulties, if we compare his performances to those few we have, including my own. In addition to his professional poise, this trainee was, as a person, always considerate of the problems at hand, and a pleasure to interact with.

I believe that these traits, although not uncommon, yet are rare enough, especially in our field which has a history of demonstrated antagonisms, personality clashes and unwillingness to comprehend the subtle natures of esp and psi. that this trainee must in some form constitute an ideal model for future selection procedures."[1]

After serving in the Army's remote viewing program from 1981-1985, Tom continued a successful career in Army counterintelligence and counterespionage. He retired from the Army in 1997.

COORDINATE REMOTE VIEWING STAGES I-VI AND BEYOND FEBRUARY 1985

TOM MCNEAR
PROJECT OFFICER

INTRODUCTION

The purpose of this document is to provide an overview of Coordinate Remote Viewing (CRV) Training Stages I through VI. CRV is the process by which a person is capable of "perceiving" information concerning a site remote from him in location and/or time given only the geographic coordinates of that location. It will provide the basics that have been learned in the past three years of training. One cannot expect to learn RV simply by reading this document. CRV must be learned by doing. Terms used in this paper peculiar to the RV process are defined in appendix A.

Stage	Example
I Major gestalt	Land surrounded by water, an island
II Sensory contact	Cold sensation, wind-swept feeling
III Dimension, motion, mobility	Rising up, panoramic view, island outline
IV General qualitative analytical aspects	Scientific research, live organisms
V Specific analytical aspects (by interrogating signal line)	Biological warfare (BW) preparation site
VI Three-dimensional contact, modeling	Layouts, details, further analytical contact
.	.
.	.
.	.

FIGURE 1
(Chart listing basics of S-I through S-VI)

CRV has been divided into discrete achievable levels called stages. Training is presented in these Stages. Each Stage is a natural progression, building on the information received from the previous Stage. These stages are tutored in order, with presentation of theory followed by a series of practical exercises taking a few weeks per stage. To learn to RV the trainee must do practical exercises in each Stage until a level of proficiency is reached. Only then can he proceed to the subsequent Stage.

The key to the lower stages of the RV process is the recognition that the major problem in attempts to remote view is the desire to visualize the site. When the viewer attempts to visualize the site he usually stimulates memory and imagination. As the viewer becomes aware of the first few data bits, there appears to be a largely spontaneous and undisciplined attempt to extrapolate and "fill in the blanks." This is presumably driven by a need to resolve the ambiguity associated with the fragmentary nature of the emerging perception (see glossary). The result is a premature internal analysis and interpretation on the part of the remote viewer. (For example, an impression of an island is immediately interpreted as Hawaii.) This is called Analytical Overlay (AOL) (see glossary).

Investigation of these overlay patterns by SRI-International led to the model of RV functioning shown in figure 2

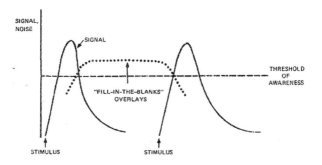

FIGURE 2 *(Schematic representation of remote viewer response to CRV situation)*

Upon receiving the stimulus, or coordinates the psychic signal reaches the threshold of awareness, the point where the signal begins to be perceptible. When the signal impacts on this threshold it is perceived by the viewer momentarily. As this signal fades away the viewer, using the first few data bits received from the initial signal, draws on memory or imagination to "create a picture" of the site. This "picture " is created from too few data bits and consequently bears little resemblance to the actual site. This is called fill-in-the-blanks overlays on the above figure. Success in handling this complex process requires the viewer to "grab" incoming data bits while simultaneously attempting to control the overlays. Stage I and Stage II training is designed to deal with this problem.

Observation of the training program indicates that remote viewing is a learnable skill. Specifically, it appears that a viewer trained in this CRV technique can be expected to exhibit a performance curve as depicted in figure 3.

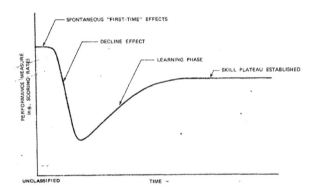

FIGURE 3 *(Idealized performance-over-time curve)*

After being exposed to the basic concepts of the training program, the vi ewer typically exhibits a few sessions of very-high quality. This is known as the "first-time effect." This quality cannot be maintained and is followed by dropping to a very low level of performance. At this point learning begins. As learning takes place, the session quality improves. Improvement continues until a plateau is reached. When this plateau is maintained for five to six consecutive sessions it is time to commence training in the next Stage.

As indicated earlier, the CRV training procedure is structured to proceed through a series of stages hypothesized to correspond to stages of increased contact with the site. These stages are tutored in order, with presentation of theory followed by a series of practical exercises taking a few weeks per stage. The viewer progresses through the stages, concentrating only on the elements to be mastered in each stage before proceeding to the next. The trainee should not be given information on stages beyond the specific stage in which he is being trained. This would challenge the trainee to progress too rapidly. Without a thorough understanding of each stage, progress into successive stages becomes very difficult.

The time required per stage is only an estimate. Training continues until the appropriate plateau is reached. The exact number of sessions is dependent on the needs of the specific viewer trainee. The quantity of sessions a trainee requires to complete a particular stage is not necessarily indicative of the his potential as a viewer. Individual differences in a trainee may impede progress in one stage while it may enhance training in other stages.

In developing this CRV training program, it was found that an experienced viewer applying the proper techniques tends to contact the site in sequential stages.

The contents of these stages are shown in figure 1, and the techniques employed are described below.

STAGE I - MAJOR GESTALT

In Stage I the viewer is trained to provide a quick-reaction response to the reading of geographic coordinates by the interviewer. The coordinates are expressed in degrees, minutes, and seconds when possible. The response takes the form of an immediate, primitive "squiggle" on paper. This "squiggle" is known as an ideogram. The ideogram captures the overall feeling/motion of the gestalt of the site (e.g., fluid /wavy for water). This response is kinesthetic and not visual. In Stage I visual images are noted and labeled as AOL.

STAGE II SENSORY CONTACT

In Stage II the viewer is trained to become sensitive to sensations associated with the site. These sensations concern sounds, smells, tastes, textures, temperatures, and energies at the site. Although colors are perceivable, Stage II signals are essentially non-visual in nature. As in Stage I, visual images are noted and declared as AOL.

STAGE III DIMENSION, MOTION, AND MOBILITY

In Stages I and II, data typically appear to emerge as fragmented data bits. In Stage III we observe the emergence of a broader concept of the site. With Stage I and II data forming a foundation, more detailed data and dimensional aspects such as length, height, and distances, begin to appear. This increased contact is known as a "widening of the aperture". At this point contact with the site appears sufficiently strengthened that the viewer begins to have an overall appreciation of the site as a whole. This is known as an "aesthetic impact". After the viewer experiences an "aesthetic impact" the urge to draw the site begins. These drawings are expressed in the form of sketches, trackers (outlines of the general configuration of the site), and additional spontaneous ideograms. The final product of Stage I through Stage III training is the recognition of the overall gestalt and physical configuration of the site.

STAGE IV - GENERAL QUALITATIVE ANALYTICAL ASPECTS

Because of the increased site contact that occurs in Stage III, in Stage IV data of an analytical nature begin to emerge. Contained in Stage IV data are elements that go beyond normal observational concepts. The ambience of the site such as military, religious, technical, or educational, can be expressed in Stage IV. Cultural factors such as Soviet, Muslim, or Arabic, and functional indicators such as power generation, my research, or human research, can also be reported accurately in Stage IV. Stage IV is therefore the point where the viewer begins to become operational.

STAGE V - SPECIFIC ANALYTICAL ASPECTS BY INTERROGATING THE SIGNAL LINE

Many complex bits of data are produced during Stage V. If during Stage IV the viewer attempts to probe or question the significance of this data it usually results in the production of AOL. The analytic functions of the viewer "try too hard" and fill in with logical but incorrect data. In Stage V however, special techniques are used to produce the more detailed information without triggering AOL.

STAGE VI - THREE DIMENSIONAL CONTACT AND MODELING

In Stage VI the viewer uses various materials to produce three dimensional representations of the site or specific elements at the site location. Materials such as clay, cardboard, and poster paper can be used to produce models of the specific structure at the site as well as the general configuration of the surrounding area. This construction is done with "feeling". The use of these materials is not simply an attempt to render a more exact representation of the site than can be done verbally, or by means of drawing. The kinesthetic activity appears to both quench AOL formation associated with purely cerebral processes, and to act as a trigger to produce further analytical content of the site, even concerning aspects not being specifically addressed by the modeling.

Detailed information concerning these training stages is included in the following chapters. Additionally, hypothesized subsequent stages are discussed later.

IDEOGRAMS

An ideogram is the kinesthetic response of the viewer to his perception of the site. Ideograms are the basis for the CRV training program. Ideograms are taught to the trainee in Stage I. Without mastering the ideogramic process the trainee cannot proceed to subsequent stages. The ideogram is the foundation for all other stages in CRV.

In CRV ideograms are produced in response of the coordinate of the site. This ideogram is viewer comes into contact with the signal line. composed of three portions:

a. The ideogram
b. A.-the feeling/motion
c. B.-the automatic analytical response

The ideogram is expressed as a "squiggle" on paper. It is produced by a spontaneous reaction of the viewer to the geographic coordinate of the site.

The viewer writes the coordinate which is spoken to him by the monitor. When this is completed he places his pen point on the paper keeping his arm relaxed so that when the unconscious, almost imperceptible, response is experienced the pen will produce a mark on the paper. This mark is the ideogram.

The second portion of the ideogram is the feeling/motion. The feeling/motion incorporates two parts. The feeling that the viewer is experiencing while he is drawing the ideogram and the mot ion that the pen makes as the ideogram is being produced. There is no single word in the English language which means both feeling and motion hence the phrase feeling/motion.

The feeling expresses the basic feeling the viewer would feel if he were actually at the site. Examples of this are: hard, fluid, manmade, smooth, etc. There are five basic categories of feelings. These are: *solid, liquid, airiness, energy, and temperature* (also a Stage II).

The motion expresses the movement of the pen as the ideogram is being produced. Examples of this are: erratic, wavy, up, down, across, etc.

It is important that the ideogram only be expressed in terms of the feeling/motion and not in terms of its visual appearance. Do not look at the ideogram and expect to see something in it.

This will lead to an AOL-DRIVE (see glossary). The feeling/motion is expressed on paper as an A- (example: A-rising solid) . This A- is on the right-central portion of the paper (see example). The final portion of the ideogram is the automatic analytical response. This is the analytical response the viewer has while or immediately after drawing the ideogram (example: land, water, building, etc.). These responses should be very general and immediate. The viewer should not "think" about producing a response. If it is not truly automatic then the viewer should simply state that there is no response. It is completely acceptable not to produce an automatic analytical response.

The automatic analytical response is expressed as a B(example: B-land). This B- should be immediately below the A-. If the viewer has no response, he should verbalize, "no B", and write B -.

There are four types of ideograms:
a. single
b. double
c. composite
d. multiple

A single ideogram is one line drawing which expresses one idea. A single ideogram should have one A - and one B -.

A - up sharp down
B - mountain

The double ideogram is a drawing of two similar lines that represent one idea which may have as many as five different parts. It may require as many as five different A's and B's.

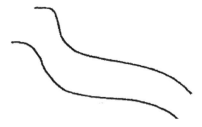

A - shifty solid
B - land

A - flowing fluid
B - water

A - hard solid
B - rock

The composite ideogram is a drawing of three or more identical or similar lines that represent one idea.
A composite ideogram should have only one A and B.

A - flowing fluid
B - waterfall

Multiple ideograms are a combination of lines which represent any number of ideas. One A- and B- is required for each idea the multiple ideogram expresses.

A - up hard down
B - mountain

A - flowing fluid
B - river

A - circling fluid
B - lake

This basic understanding of ideograms is necessary before proceeding to the following chapters. Following discusses the six Stage CRV process in detail.

STAGE I
MAJOR GESTALT

Stage I is the most important stage in the CRV training program. Stage I is also the most difficult to train. Stage I is the basis for the entire CRV process.

In chapter 2 we discussed Ideograms and how they are formed. The ideogram initially appears to provide little data. However, with more detailed inspection one finds the ideogram posses all the basic information necessary to proceed on to the operational data that we require. This information is contained in the feeling/motion of the ideogram.

In teaching CRV we are not teaching the trainee to be psychic. We are not teaching him to receive the signal. We are teaching him the proper format to be used in objectifying the data he perceives upon receiving the coordinate. This is known as the session "Structure". In this CRV technology we believe that as long as the viewer maintains proper control of his structure the data can be considered generally correct. It must be stressed to the viewer at all times that only by monitoring his structure can he know the value or correctness of the data he is producing. The best results are produced when the viewer ignores the content of the data and concentrates on the structure. This structure is always controlled by the viewer.

The following information concerning session structure is an integral part of Stage I. Structure and Stage I must be taught concurrently, hence a large portion of this chapter is devoted to structure. However, the structure learned in Stage I is used throughout the CRV process.

Structure is broken into two areas:

> **1.** The interaction of the interviewer and viewer.

> **2.** The proper sequences of steps taken by the viewer
> to grasp the ideograms and objectify the data.

The interaction of the interviewer and viewer should be kept to a minimum to prevent inadvertent cuing or extemporaneous stimulus which might interfere with the viewer's ability to retrieve and objectify the signal. In objectifying the signal the viewer expresses, on paper, the perceptions or processes taking place in his head. All superfluous talking should be saved for the completion of the session. The date/time, coordinates or alternate cuing data, and specific feedback statements are the only inputs the monitor should make during the conduct of the session.

There are three classes of CRV sessions. These classes deal with the feed-back given or not given to the viewer during the session. These three classes: A, B, and C, are discussed next.

PROTOCOLS

CLASS C
- Used in training sessions
- Monitor is knowledgeable of the site; therefore session
  carried out under non-blind conditions.
- Intersession feedback given to facilitate learning process.
 - Session results do not stand alone as proof-of-principle
  because of cueing possibilities.
- Evaluation of RV results inapplicable; performance curve
  measures, e.g., number of coordinate iterations required,
  only.

CLASS B
 - Used in confirmation, evaluation.
 - Monitor is blind to site.
 - Feedback given only post-session.
 - Statistical techniques applicable to RV accuracy
   assessment.

CLASS A
- Used in operational RV, simulations.
- Monitor is blind in majority of cases; non-blind analysts or
  observers occasionally present.
- Feedback conditions variable, depending on task

requirements.

- Evaluation techniques as determined by user.

The majority of the training sessions are Class C, with feedback. It is during training the viewer trainee must learn to differentiate between the emerging signal and AOL. This is done by immediate feedback during training.

To begin a session in Stage I the viewer trainee writes his name, location, and interviewers' name on the upper right corner of the paper. When this is complete

the interviewer states the date/time group and the viewer writes this below the other information. This administrative data objectifies, in the mind of the viewer, the conditions (date, time, and location) for the beginning of the session. The coordinates objectify the specific site for that session . The viewers job is to, through proper structure control, describe the objects and activities at that site.

After this is accomplished the viewer momentarily checks himself for any problems, physical or emotional, which might interfere with his ability to RV. These inhibiting factors are called personal inclemency's (PI). All PI should be declared and objectified by writing it across the top of the page (example: PI- experiencing back pain). When problems are being experienced with bodily functions, the mind is preoccupied and the viewer cannot give his complete attention to the task at hand. If the PI is such that it may cause too much attenuation of the signal, then, if possible, the session should be aborted. When the PI is no longer a factor then the session can be attempted.

When the viewer feels confident and ready to grasp the signal he places his pen on the paper in the appropriate place for the coordinates. Upon seeing this, the monitor reads the coordinates slowly to the viewer who writes them.

Immediately after writing the coordinates, the signal will present itself in the form of an ideogram. The A-(feeling/motion) for each part of the ideogram is stated orally to the interviewer as it is objectified on the paper. The B- (automatic analytical response), if present, is also declared both orally and in writing. If no B- is present, this too should be declared. This is considered a completed Stage I sequence. Ideally the ideogram and the A- produce a B - (I+A=B).

The coordinates may be restated any number of times, at the viewers discretion. After an I, A, B sequence is completed, the next reading of the coordinate should produce a different, more detailed, ideogram. Only after the I, A, B sequence is properly completed, however, will this new ideogram come. If during this process the same ideogram is produced with each iteration of the coordinate it indicates the ideogram has been incompletely or incorrectly interpreted. This means the viewer must take more care in producing the A-(feeling /motion). Often after the A- has been thoroughly expressed the viewer will be able to provide a B-. Once the ideogram has been correctly interpreted the next ideogram will present itself.

Ideograms come in sequential order from the main gestalt of the site to the smaller details. When an ideogram is correctly and completely interpreted another will present itself offering more information about the site.

The example below indicates the proper Stage I format and is considered a completed Stage I session.

VIEWER NAME
FT MEADE
INTERVIEWER NAME
DATE/TIME GROUP

37° 43I 17.2 N
122° 42I 11.8 E

A-rising
hard
B-mountain

Each consecutive entry on the paper is entered below the previous entry. This provides a chronological history of the data. If, during the session it is noted that the viewer is out of structure, this chronological history will allow him to review the data and to correct the structure. At the conclusion of the session, an analyst, by reviewing the session structure, can know the reliability of the data.

During Class C (training) sessions the interviewer will provide the viewer with immediate feed-back for each element of data the viewer provides. This feed-back, in order to prevent inadvertent cuing, is in the form of very specific statements. These statements and their definitions follow:

Site (S)
This indicates the site has been correctly named for the specific stage being trained (manmade structure for Stage I, bridge for Stage III). Site indicates that the session is completed.

Correct (C)
This indicates that the information is correct in context with the site location, but is not sufficient to end the session.

Probably Correct (PC)
This statement means that the interviewer, due to limited feed-back materials, while not sure, believes that the information provided is correct.

Near (N)
This indicates that the information provided is not an element of the specific site, but is correct for the immediate surrounding area.

Can't Feed-back (CFB)
This statement indicates that, due to limited feed-back materials, the interviewer cannot make a judgment as to the correctness of the data. It means neither correct nor incorrect.

Negative feed-back is not given. When the viewer incorrectly states an element of information no feed-back is given.

During the session the viewer writes the abbreviation (see above) of the feed-back next' to the data. This allows the viewer, during training, to review the correct elements and produce a summary which describes the site. The session continues, during training, until the interviewer responds with the feedback of Site.

At any time during the session or upon completion of the session, the viewer can complete a summary of the information he has produced. This often is helpful in creating a "picture" of the site in the mind of the viewer. During all sessions beyond Stage IV, and for all operational sessions a summary should be included at the end. This summary should be written in the words of the viewer and should include all data which was produced during the session.

When the viewer provides the required detail for the session to be considered complete the interviewer will indicate this by feeding back, site, end. The viewer objectifies this on the paper below the last entry on the paper. When this is complete the interviewer states the time for the completion of the session and this, too, is written by the viewer.

To this point we have discussed the ideal session, but what happens when things don't go ideally? We have a method for handling that too. When things are going well we keep working, but when they aren't we take breaks.

There are specific types of breaks and appropriate times to take them. When a break is taken the viewer objectifies the type of break on the paper and orally. The

reason the viewer called the break is also stated and

written. The brakes and when to use them follows:

BREAK

A break can be taken anytime the viewer feels the need. This break should not be taken, however, when the signal is flowing smoothly. If the break is going to be more than a pause this should be indicated (example: 5 minute break). If the break is an extended break the ending time should be annotated on the paper and the resume date/time should be entered (example: Resume-date/time).

MISS BREAK

A miss break is taken anytime the viewer misses the ideogram after the presentation of the coordinates. A miss break can also be taken if the viewer misses the feeling and/or the motion. The miss break is beneficial in that it tells the system that the signal was missed and to stop looking for it. If this is not done the brain will produce an AOL rather than admit it missed it. After a moment's pause the viewer should retake the coordinates and proceed. Any number of miss breaks can be called. There is no shame in missing the signal, the shame is in not calling the break and allowing AOL to be produced.

AOL BREAK

An AOL break is called any time the viewer realizes he has received an AOL. The viewer should call an AOL Break and objectify the AOL (example: AOL Break- Devil's Tower). This break acknowledges that it was an AOL and objectifies it to clear it from the system. The viewer should remain on break until the AOL "goes away".

This may take a few seconds or a few minutes. There

are times, however, the AOL may linger and consequently an extended break may be appropriate. AOL are recognized by three methods:

1. If the signal becomes a bright, motionless, visual image it is considered an AOL.

2. If the data is qualified it is considered an AOL. Statements such as: it is like ... , I think it's, ... , or maybe it's ... , are all AOL. It is also considered an AOL if there is a stutter, pause, or hesitation accompanying the data.

3. If the statement is totally unjustified by the previous data it is considered an AOL. , An example is if the viewer has an A- of rising hard and calls the site water.

AOL DRIVE BREAK (AOL-D break)
An AOL-D break is similar to an AOL break except that an AOL-D indicates that the viewer did not call an AOL break in time and has been working with an AOL. This AOL is "driving" the system, hence the name. When the viewer realizes he is operating with a AOL-D he must go back in this data and locate the AOL, declare it, and break it from the system. All data from that point is suspect and should not be relied upon. With an AOL-D a longer break is usually required.

BI-LOCATION BREAK (BILO Break)
To properly RV a site the viewer must be hi-located, that is, he must have his perceptions at the site while still occupying physical space in the viewing room. When the viewer realizes he is not maintaining this bi-location he must call a BILO Break. If the viewer

is too much in the viewing room, as evidenced by chit-chat with the interviewer, he will not be perceiving much data from the site. Conversely if he is too into the site, as evidenced by long periods of silence, he will be perceiving the data but he won't be reporting it. After a momentary break the viewer should pick up where he left off.

TOO MUCH BREAK (TM Break)

A TM Break is called when the viewer receives too much data to debrief. If he tries to work through it a confusion will 11 result. After a short break the viewer should continue from where he left off.

CONFUSION BREAK (CONF Break)

A CONF Break is called anytime the viewer is confused. Without acknowledging this confusion the viewer may incorporate the confusion into the session. The viewer should declare the confusion and objectify it so it can be removed from the system. A break should be taken until the confusion is gone.

By the use of appropriate breaks the viewer is able to control his structure. As we have stated earlier, it is the control of structure that we are actually teaching.

Stage I is taught in two phases. Stage I, phase I uses coordinates that represent only one large gestalt. Examples of this are large mountain ranges, large cities, and coordinates in the middle of the ocean. Stage I phase I are more detailed sites such as rivers through mount a in ranges, cities on the ocean, or small islands.

STAGE II
SENSORY CONTACT

In Stage I, the signal line is noticeably of brief duration and extremely narrow in aperture. As the viewer continues in contact with the signal line, however, the aperture widens somewhat, and a broader, slower signal is received. This signal consists of those sensations/feelings which the viewer might bodily experience were he physically at the site. These sensations are the signals processed during Stage II. Such basic things as tastes, smells, tactile sensations such as: textures, sounds, colors, temperatures, and energies such as: magnetics, radiation, electricity, etc. are received in Stage II. Stage II is unique in that the sensations produced usually generate little or no AOL because they are fundamental data bits that require no analysis or interpretation by the brain. These data bits, which are informally designate "Stage I Is", present themselves in clusters upon the proper decoding of the ideogram, A., B. sequence.

A cluster of Stage IIs may consist of two or more sensations. A single Stage II is called a "floating Stage II" and is not as reliable as those that come in "clusters". These clusters tend to represent different aspects of the site, i.e. a cluster for a building, for surrounding terrain, for water present at the site, or some other significant geographical or artificial feature, etc. Separate series of Stage IIs may be obtained for each separate I, A., B. sequence.

After the viewer has produced a B- (or acknowledged there is no B-), the Stage II signals may begin to flow. To objectify these signals the viewer writes "S-2" on the mid-point of the paper (see example below), and writes the Stage II signals, in column form, as they present themselves.

The process of aperture expansion seems to function on a continuum, and as one progresses into Stage II, the aperture widens. This produces a new category of Stage I Is known as dimensionals. These dimensionals are the beginning of Stage III and are discussed in the next chapter.

Because Stage II signals are mostly normal bodily sensations which we experience daily, Stage II is one of the easiest and fastest stages to teach.

Stage II signals at first seem to lack any real value.

They are extremely basic and express little about the true nature of the site. It is important to realize the viewer must progress through the Stage II signals before he will experience a "widening of the aperture". This expanded contact with the site leads, as is discussed in the next chapter, to aesthetic impact which is the element of CRV which truly leads to the production of information of intelligence value.

STAGE III
DIMENSION, MOTION, AND MOBILITY

As discussed earlier, the purpose of Stage I is to teach the viewer the proper session structure and to train him to produce ideograms and process As and Bs. Stage II teaches the viewer to process sensations perceived from the site. Using the data produced by these Stages as a base the viewer can move into Stage III. Stage III allows the viewer to achieve a broader, more dimension a 1 contact with the site. This improved contact allows the viewer to sketch the physical characteristics of the site. Stage III is broken into five separate components which are taught as a package. However, the ultimate goal of Stage III is TOTAL COMMAND OF STRUCTURE.

Stage III is composed of five elements:

1. Aesthetic Impact (AI):
An AI is the point where the viewer is so overwhelmed with his perceptions of the site that he is unable to report them. An AI occurs after three to four dimensional descriptors are reported in Stage II. An AI is indicated by a shift in the viewers' mood or

emotion. An AI is defined as a statement which describes how the site makes the viewer feel, or how the viewer feels about the site, i.e. lonely, magnificent, or "don't like it here". AI is one of the more difficult aspects of CRV to understand and express. Some AIs can be very powerful, some very weak, and some very subtle. The AI must be recognized and declared as AI BREAK. If an AI goes undeclared it can produce AOL colored by AI, bringing about AOL-Drive or peacocking (see glossary). AI are produced after the viewer has reported dimensionals, which indicates a change in aperture has occurred. After the viewer gets four or more dimensionals, he should look for the AI, although it may occur after only two or three. Dimensionals will be forced from Stage II until an appropriate AI is declared. If the AI keeps coming back it has not been correctly resolved. The viewer must return to where the AI was first experienced and inspect it to see how it made them "feel". This feeling should then be expressed as an AI Break. This corrected AI will produce better site contact and in turn lead to the other elements of Stage III.

2. Enhanced Dimensional Contact:

A dimension is an extension in a single line or direction as length, breadth, thickness, or depth. A line has one dimension: length. A plane has two dimensions: length and breadth. A solid has 3 dimensions: length, breadth, and thickness. A dimension is an aspect of the site. Dimensionality is dependent on the view point of the viewer and is not an aspect of the site. Dimensions are expressed as:

a. Horizontal: A horizontal line is parallel to the horizon, opposite of vertical.

b. Vertical: A vertical line is perpendicular to the horizon, the opposite of horizontal.

c. Diagonal: A diagonal line is the point of intersection of two lines of a figure. A diagonal is neither vertical nor horizontal.

d. Mass: A quantity of matter that forms a body of indefinite shape; usually matter. Whatever forms a body is usually made up of matter. Mass indicates overall size.

e. Volume: Volume is a quantity, bulk, mass, or amount. The addition of mass or volume provides a third dimension to the site. This indicates a change in aperture, and should produce an AI. If the AI is not present, the viewer may need another dimension.

f. Space: The absence of any of the above. Empty distance; an interval between things.

MOTION AND MOBILITY:
Motion is the act or process of moving; the passage of a body from one place to another. Mot ion is used to describe movement of things at the site.

Mobility is the state or quality of being mobile. Mobility indicates that the viewer has the ability to be mobile, or move at the site.

TRACKERS:
Trackers are like a very detailed ideogram, but instead of being a solid line, a tracker is formed by dots. A tracker is drawn very slowly using dots because it is the viewer's autonomic system making the decision of where the next dot should go, and not his conscious processing. Generally, a tracker will accurately follow the configuration of the site.

Dimensions are required to produce a tracker.

SKETCHES:

A sketch is a general outline without much detail. It is drawn more slowly than an ideogram but faster than a tracker and is used to express an idea. Sketches produced immediately after an ideogram are out of structure and are considered AOL. Sketches are drawn after an appropriate AI. It is mobility that allows the production of sketches.

Sketches can be drawn both while in and out of contact with the signal. Sketches drawn while in contact with the signal are drawn rapidly and spontaneously.

Sketches drawn while out of contact with the signal are premeditated and analytically produced using a prescribed format.

To produce an analytic sketch of the site the viewer works through dimensional descriptors until an appropriate AI is produced. The viewer then lists his data in three categories: dimensionals, secondary elements, and details. Next, using the above listed elements, the viewer deliberately creates an analytical drawing starting with the horizontal elements, then the vertical elements, and finally the diagonal (angular) elements. After this is done the secondary elements and details are filled in.

Regardless of which method of sketching is used, at no time should the viewer be sketching an image he has in his head. The sketches should be created from pre-visual information. If the viewer has an image in his head it should be declared AOL and an appropriate break should be taken.

While producing sketches, by either method, the viewer must be alert for spontaneous ideograms which may be produced. The viewer can recognize a spontaneous ideogram by the speed or "automaticness" with which it was produced. When this occurs the viewer should attempt to produce an A and B. If there is an A present, then this portion of the sketch was a spontaneous ideogram. During the Stage III training session, the coordinate prompts the ideogram, which prompts the A and B, which prompts Stage I Is (including dimensions), which prompt the AI, which prompts mobility, which prompts trackers and sketches.

During Stage III the viewer can be moved to different times and locations. Because RV is a passive activity the phrases used to prompt mobility should be in the passive form. Cuing such as "300 feet north something should be perceptible" is used because it doesn't require an active response of the viewer.

While increased site contact is the more interesting element of Stage III, it is secondary to the real goal of Stage III. Again, THE PRIMARY GOAL OF STAGE III IS TOTAL COMMAND OF STRUCTURE. To complete Stage III the viewer must deliver a rendering of the ideogram, Stage I and Stage II to include at least three dimensionals, recognize and debrief an appropriate AI, become mobile at and around the site, and possibly produce a tracker or sketch, ALL WITH PROPER STRUCTURE CONTROL.

STAGE IV
GENERAL QUALITATIVE ANALYTICAL ASPECTS

Whereas Stages I through III are directed toward recognition of the overall gestalt and physical configuration of the site, Stage IV goes beyond descriptions of the physical attributes of the site. Stage IV describes activities and objects at the site as well the feelings and emotions people at the site are experiencing. Because of this increased contact with the site, Stage IV is considered to be the threshold for operational utility.

In Stage IV the trainee is instructed to separate the incoming data into eight different categories. These categories are described below.

Stage II (S-2)
These are the same sensations which were discussed in chapter four. These signals, while still classified as Stage II because of their nature, are often more detailed because of the increased contact of Stage IV. Examples are: blue, hard, car smells, etc.

Dimensionals (D)

Dimensional signals describe the physical size of elements at the site. These are similar to the dimensionals of Stage III, but are usually more detailed. Examples are: tall, thin, 350 feet, etc.

Aesthetic Impact (AI)

This is the column where the viewer debriefs his AI. This is a close-ended column which means the viewer still takes an AI Break as in Stage III and stops participating in the signal. Examples are: "WOW, this place makes me feel wonderful!"

Emotional Impact (EI)

Emotional impacts are signals the viewer receives from people at the site. Any time a viewer perceives people at the site he should immediately move to this column and look for EI signals. These signals are very revealing as to what is occurring at the site. This is an open-ended column, the viewer should not call a break, instead he should continue to participate with these signals. The EI signal is a very slow signal. The viewer should take his time when debriefing EI, there is no need to ca 11 a BILO Break while waiting for EI. Examples of EI are: sad, happy, remorse, etc.

Tangibles (T)

A tangible object is something which can be touched. This column is use to report "things" at the site. Examples are: trees, buildings, people, chairs, etc.

Intangibles (I)

Intangible signals are those that are not tangible or touchable. Examples of signals which should be put in this column are: religious, military, Soviet, etc.

AOL

In this column the viewer reports all AOL. This is a close-ended column. As with all AOL the viewer will call an AOL-Break and stop participating with the signal. An example is the remembrance of a place which reminds the viewer of the perceptions he is reporting.

AOL From The Signal (A/S)

While A/Sis not necessarily the site, it is not a true AOL. AOL from the signal is a hazy image which is still considered pre-visual. It is an analytical construct of the viewers mind. These A/S will be reported in the A/S column. No break will be called because the viewer should continue to participate in this signal. The viewer must be aware this A/S can become an AOL and be ready to transfer it into the AOL column. Example: If the site is a radio tower, but the viewer receives an A/ S of the Eifel Tower, the signal is an A/ S instead of an AOL. It is trying to show the viewer the site "looks like" the Eifel Tower.

The above items are written across the top of each page after the session progresses into Stage IV. Below is a sample Stage IV format:

S-2	D	AI	EI	T	I	AOL
A/S						

This "matrix" is written by the viewer rather than using a pre-printed format. Writing the matrix cues the viewer kinesthetically, in each column, each time it is written.

The information being debriefed should flow back-and-forth across the page. The viewer should ensure that information is being placed in each column. If he sees that one or more columns are being neglected he should prompt those columns to ensure that no information is being admitted. To prompt, the viewer simply places his pen point in the appropriate column. This should cause a flow of data to be received in that category.

When the viewer produces a T he should attempt to sketch it. If, during Stage IV a spontaneous sketch is produced the viewer should attempt to debrief it for Ts.

This is an important aspect which leads to tremendous quantities of data. This often requires reinforcement during the session.

To complete Stage IV the viewer must:

1. be able to produce sufficient quantities of data in each column while maintaining proper session control.

2. produce sketches from T's and T's from sketches.

It is important for the viewer to be able to confidently produce information in Stage IV. Often the viewer will produce data bits which seem to make   little   sense.

The viewer should not spend time trying to analyze this information, in Stage IV this will only result in producing AOL. In Stage V the viewer will learn to interrogate these signals for details without producing AOL.

STAGE V
SPECIFIC ANALYTICAL ASPECTS BY
INTERROGATING THE SIGNAL LINE

Stage IV produces large quantities of information, however many times this information is too complex or confusing for the Stage IV proficient viewer to deal with. Attempts to investigate this data in Stage IV usually ends in the production of AOL. It is Stage V that allows the viewer to "interrogate" (see glossary) the signals to get the appropriate detail without producing AOL. Additionally, Stage V is considered a corrective action stage in that it allows the viewer to "look through" AOL and find the data which caused the production of the AOL. There are many valuable signals lying under AOL.

Stage V offers exciting possibilities for intelligence collection. Whereas Stage IV can identify a site as being a library, Stage V allows the viewer to "enter the library" by interrogating the signal line and identify the subject of the books being maintained in the library. This allows the viewer to differentiate between a legal library and an art, or S&T library.

Stage V allows the viewer to interrogate the signal line regarding the categories of objects, attributes, subjects, and topics of the site. First we will define these categories and give examples of each and then we will discuss the actual technique used to interrogate the signal line.

OBJECT

An object, according to the dictionary, is anything that is visible or tangible and is stable in form. When the viewer prompts for objects he should expect to perceive objects related to the signal being interrogated. Examples of objects are: buildings, tanks, weapons, people, etc.

ATTRIBUTE

The definition of an attribute is: something seen as belonging to or representing someone or something. When the viewer produces data of interest, it can be interrogated for its attributes. Example: the attributes of a school are: books, students, desks, rooms, teachers, etc.

SUBJECT

A subject is a matter or topic that forms the basis of a conversation, train of thought, investigation, etc. An element of data can be interrogated for the underlying subjects. Example: The subjects of a school are: education, learning, languages, etc.

TOPIC

A topic is a subject of conversation or discussion. A topic is more detailed than a subject; subjects have topics. The subject of languages has the topics of: grammar, German, English, etc.

While the concept of objects and attributes can be easily understood, the concept of subjects and topics is not. Objects and their attributes are tangible and exist. People deal with these ideas daily. Subjects and topics are not tangible, however. The dividing line between a subject and a topic is very hazy. Because of this, a large portion of Stage V training is devoted towards this concept. In the past it has taken several days of drills to instill this understanding in the viewer. In spite of this difficulty however, once the viewer truly understands the relationship between subject and topic it is no longer a problem and training proceeds very rapidly.

Now that the categories have been defined, it is important to understand the relationship between them. Basically, objects have attributes and attributes have objects; subjects have topics and topics have subjects. However, any item of data can be interrogated in any of the above categories.

We have mentioned prompting. What is prompting? In order to interrogate any piece of data the viewer merely writes the word, statement, or phrase to be interrogated on the next available space on the paper. He then writes below this the category he wishes to interrogate for. For example, if he wants the attributes of an object he writes the name of the object and below this he writes "attributes".

When this is done the word "emanations?"(with a question mark) is written below the category and the information will become available to him. The word emanate means: to flow out, issue, or proceed, as to come from a source or origin. When we prompt for emanations in any category we are merely asking if there is any signal to be received. This does not lead to AOL. A question of, "Are there any people there", would force the viewer into a yes or no situation which could easily induce AOL. When we ask for emanations we are not doing so with a preconceived idea (such as people). We are simply taking whatever response we receive from the prompt. If, when prompted, the data does not produce any information in that category, simply try another category. Below is an example:

building
attributes
emanations?
> *tall*
> *brown*
> *people*
> *glass*
> *concrete*
> *etc.*

Building can also be interrogated for its subjects:

building
subjects
emanations?
> *knowledge*
> *learning*
> *students*
> *the arts*
> *etc.*

As you can see, when building was interrogated for subjects, the objects of "students" and the topic of "the arts", came out. This is considered normal. The interrogation will sometimes automatically shift over to a different category. As long as the information continues to flow the viewer should continue to accept it.

The best time to begin Stage V is when the signal slows or stops in Stage IV. During operational sessions, when the interviewer sees an item of particular interest he may, at that time, request the viewer to interrogate it for more information. When the Stage IV signal stops the viewer should review his data for elements which have the greatest potential for interrogation. Generally, object being interrogated for attributes or subjects is the best place. This is because the EEI we are attempting to answer is usually concerned with "things".

As previously stated, Stage V can be used to "look through AOL" to find the raw data which caused the AOL. There is usually a lot of signal incorporated into the AOL. To retrieve this information the viewer writes the AOL and then interrogates for the "prior emanations" or the information which preceded the AOL. An example follows.

If the viewer had an AOL of the Empire State Building, he should do the following.

Empire State Building
  prior emanations?
    tall
    angular
    massive
     gray
     etc.

To complete Stage V the viewer must master the

ability to review his data, to select the best "leads", and to move freely between categories.

An analysis of an actual Stage V session is included on the next page. In this session the site was US Grants Farm, outside St Louis, Missouri. This shows the order in which the information flowed during the session.

As previously stated, Stage V offers exciting possibilities for intelligence collection. It allows the viewer, without AOL, to glean tremendous amounts of information from the session. With Stage V completed the viewer is ready to move into Stage VI or three dimensional modeling of the site which allows the analyst to see what the viewer is "seeing".

STAGE VI
THREE DIMENSIONAL CONTACT
AND MODELING

As previously stated Stage III allows the viewer to sketch the general physical configuration of the site. Stage VI is a continuation of the expression of the sites physical characteristics. In Stage VI the viewer, using various modeling materials, will construct a three dimensional model of the site or a montage of the site area to include natural and manmade elements. These models can be very accurate. A Stage VI model is a tangible form of information which can be very helpful when given to analyst. A Stage VI model of the building in which a hostage is being held would very beneficial in locating him.

These models are constructed from "feel" and not by simply modeling the Stage III sketch. It is important to understand the modeling process is not simply an attempt to render a more exact representation of the site than can be done verbally, or by means of drawing. Stage VI modeling is a kinesthetic activity which appears to both quench the desire to produce

AOL and it acts as cuing to produce further analytical content of the site, even concerning aspects of the site not being specifically addressed by the modeling.

Stage VI is a very easy stage to teach. The viewer simply takes clay (or whatever materials he is using), and proceeds to construct, to the best of his physical abilities, a three dimensional model of the site. When this is done he should move his hands (and perceptions) around the area surrounding the model and "feel" for anything that may be located near the site. If "something is located he can model it, sketch it on the mounting board in its approximate location, or he can return to the paper and go for ideograms of this "unknown something". During the Stage VI modeling process the viewer must continue to objectify, on paper, any verbiage or ideograms which he may produce.

It is recommended that the viewer trainee spend some time working with the modeling materials before ever beginning a session. This experience will make it easier for him to model during the session and allow him to keep his attention on the session and not on the mechanics of modeling. Modeling ability quickly improves with time and practice.

Stage VI is an exciting and fun stage for the viewer and interviewer alike. The physical model represents the culmination of a long training process and can give the viewer a tremendous feeling of accomplishment.

This is the completion of the six stage training program as was developed by I. Swann. The next chapter deals with hypothesized follow-on stages and attempts to give the reader an idea of where CRV can take us.

SAMPLE CRV SESSION
STAGES I-VI

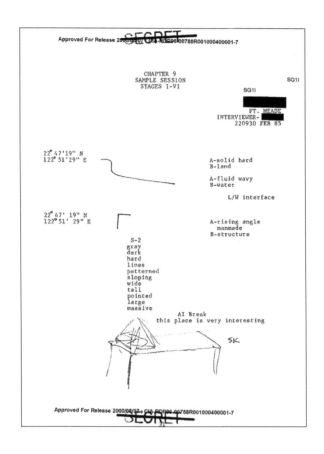

CHAPTER 9
SAMPLE SESSION
STAGES I-VI

SG1I

SG1I

FT. MEADE
INTERVIEWER-
220930 FEB 85

22° 47'19" N
122° 51'29" E

A-solid hard
B-land

A-fluid wavy
B-water

L/W interface

22° 47' 19" N
122° 51' 29" E

A-rising angle
    manmade
B-structure

S-2
gray
dark
hard
lines
patterned
sloping
wide
tall
pointed
large
massive

AI Break
this place is very interesting

SK

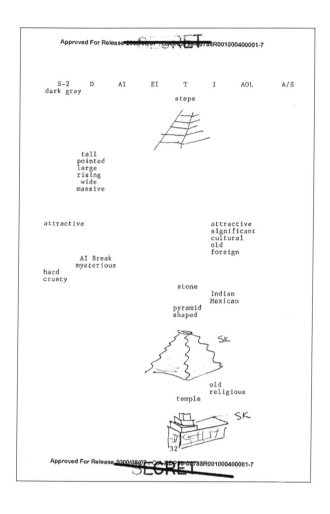

S-2   D   AI   EI   T   I   AOL   A/S
dark gray
                                steps

                    tall
                    pointed
                    large
                    rising
                    wide
                    massive

attractive   attractive
                                        significant
                                        cultural
                                        old
                                        foreign

                AI Break
                mysterious
hard
crusty
                                stone
                                        Indian
                                        Mexican
                                pyramid
                                shaped

                                                SK

                                        old
                                        religious
                                temple

                                                SK

                                32

83

CRV - CONTROLLED REMOTE VIEWING

STAGE 5
```
        temple
        attributes
        emanations?
         hard
          rising
       straight
        gray
         stone
        massive
```
```
                                   significant
                                    subject
                                    emanations?
                                    important
                                    central
                                    historical
                                    large
                                    hard
                                     rising
```
```
      significant
       objects
      emanations?
       hard
       rising
       tall
       foreign
      Mexican
```

STAGE VI
      (The next is a photo of the Stage VI model which was produced.)

STAGE VII
      (The following phonetic sounds were produced.)
```
                                   oo
                                   to
                                   tooo
                                   lu
                                   toolu
                                   tooloo
```
```
                    the site is the the Mayan Temple
                              at Tolum
```
```
                         SITE    END
                          1017
```

SECRET
UNCLASSIFIED

(a) SITE

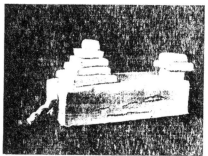

UNCLASSIFIED

(b) RV RESPONSE

FIGURE 2   (U)   TULUM RUINS, MEXICO

11

FUTURE STAGES

This chapter deals with possible future stages. These stages are the personal thoughts of the writer. They are the product of the last three and one-half years of training and work in the area of CRV. These ideas are my own, however, they were developed from many hours of thought and discussion with other people with common interests.

During this training program it has become apparent there is a natural progression, or continuum, to the psychic signal. This progression continues beyond RV, to the ability to exert ones influence over persons and things at the site. The following stages, I believe, follow this natural progression. By calling them stages, I am not implying they are trainable. I am merely stating they appear to fit into the natural flow of the signal.

STAGE VII ANALYTICS

Analytics is the ability to make a yes/no decision without producing AOL. This also gives the viewer the ability to "recognize" numbers and letters. This is a further development of Stages IV and V. This has application in the recognition of addresses in search problems and code breaking. This stage is in the process of development by I. Swann. According to Mr. Swann this development is proceeding well.

STAGE VIII PHONETICS/SONICS

This, too, is a concept of I. Swann. This was originally believed to be Stage VII until he realized analytics actually preceded it. Stage VIII will allow the viewer to produce phonetic I sonic sounds which, it is hypothesized, will allow the viewer to produce the name of persons, places, and things at the site. In my experience these signals, which I have produced, have at times been very accurate. An example of this is "Carr ibah", which was produced when tasked against Karriba Dam.

STAGE IX TELEPATHIC SIGNALS

Stage IX is a follow-on to the Stage IV emotional impact (EI) column. The EI column is the place the viewer discusses the "feelings" of people at the site. If the viewer is "in-touch" with a distant per sons feelings the next step would seem to be a more complete telepathic link. Stage IX would be broken into two phases:

PHASE I
would be receiving telepathic signals from the site area. Again, this is very similar to Stage IV

EI.

PHASE II
would be transmitting telepathic signals to the site area. Once we understand telepathic signals well enough to receive them the next step would be to transmit them.

STAGE X REMOTE ACTION (RA)

Stage X would be mind-over-matter, also known as psychokinesis (PK). We have very little understanding of PK, but we do know it exists. If Stage IX is telepathic signals which effect people, it is logical the next stage would be RA signals which effect "things". Stage X would be divided into three phases:

PHASE I
would be affecting or interacting with "things" at the site.

PHASE II
would be teleportation of things from the site. Teleportation is an element of PK. Once we can interact with things at the site the next step would be to "bring things back from the site".

PHASE III
would be teleportation of things to the site. Once we can remove things from the site we should be able to send them as well.

STAGE XI ALTERING THE DIMENSIONALITY AT THE SITE

This is the most difficult stage to understand. Time is considered another dimension, but there may be many more. Mathematically it is considered that there are infinite numbers of dimensions. Stage XI would be broken into at least two phases:

PHASE I
would be altering time at the site. Time could be frozen, moved forward, or moved back. The implications of this are mind boggling. I believe this is the first stage where we could truly effect (alter) the future (as well as the past and the present).

PHASE II
Maybe by the time we reach Stage XI we will understand enough about alternate dimensions to use this phase. I believe there would probably be an additional phase for each additional dimension we discover.

I realize these concepts are difficult to grasp and impossible to believe, but, they are a natural flow of the signal and it is for this reason I included them.

Only time will tell, whatever time is.

CONCLUSIONS

After four years of training I know the CRV training program is a usable program for instructing personnel to RV. As we increase our data base and understanding we are finding the time required for training can be shortened. If the instructors are a dedicated group who truly understand CRV this program will continue to improve and expand.

Future stages will continue to develop, I believe, in the general order which I presented them in the previous chapter The future of CRV is only limited by the imagination and efforts of the people pursuing it.

I believe we establish our own realities of what will and won't work. We once had a viewer who believed he could view, but he couldn't view different time zones, consequently he succeeded as a viewer, but failed as a "time traveler". His reality would not allow him to accomplish the same tasks as his peers, simply because he didn't believe.

It is imperative the personnel working in this office

keep an open mind and be allowed to pursue new and sometimes radical ideas. The more radical efforts may produce the most gain in the long run.

APPENDIX A
GLOSSARY

A- A label representing the feeling motion.

Aesthetic - Keenly responsive to and appreciative of beauty in art, nature, etc.

Aesthetic Impact (AI) - So keenly appreciative or aware of the site that the individual is unable to describe his perceptions.

Analysis - A method of determining the nature of a thing by separating it into its parts; separating the feeling motion from the ideogram in order to determine the B - or site.

Analytical Overlay (AOL) - Information produced by the conscious or unconscious which clutters the signal; noise.

AOL Drive (AOL-D) - The viewer is in AOL-D when he has failed to acknowledge an AOL and it is "driving" the session. Automatic - Occurring independently of volition; involuntary.

Aware - Informed, alert, knowledgeable.

B - A label representing the automatic analysis of the feeling motion and the ideogram.

Break - To terminate a mission for a period of time.

Can't Feed-back (CFB) - This statement indicates that, due to limited feed-back materials, the interviewer cannot make a judgment as to the correctness of the data. It means neither correct nor incorrect.

Conscious - Aware of one's own existence, thoughts, surroundings, etc.

Confusion (CON) - A statement of being perplexed.

Correct (C) - This indicates that the information is correct in context with the site location, but is not sufficient to end the session.

Feeling Motion - A feeling and motion combined, a feeling of motion.

Gestalt - A configuration having specific properties that cannot be derived from the summation of its parts. The concept that the whole is greater than the sum of its parts.

Idea - Any conception existing in the mind as a result of mental understanding, awareness or activity.

Ideogram - A written symbol that represents an

idea.

Impact - To make an impression.

Interviewer - The individual who assists the viewer during a CRV session.

Interrogate - To question, as in questioning the signal line.

Miss - To fail to capture the signal.

Near (N) - This indicates that the information provided is not an element of the specific site, but is correct for the immediate surrounding area.

Noiseless - Accompanied by or making no noise, a mission free of AOL.

Objectify - To present as an object, externalize, to write on paper.

Objective - Something that one's efforts are intended to attain.

Peacocking - Peacocking is when the analytical portion of the viewer's brain tries to assist in identifying the site. The product of this assistance is an endless stream of AOL.

Perception - The act or faculty of apprehending information by means of the senses or the mind, cognition, or understanding.

Probably Correct (PC) - This statement means that the interviewer, due to the limited feed-back materials, while not sure, believes that the information provided is correct.

Signal - The signal is the means by which the information is received by the viewer.

Site (S) - This indicates that the site has been correctly named for the specific stage being trained (manmade structure for Stage I, bridge for Stage III). Site indicates that the session is completed.

Structure - The manner in which the mission is to be conducted.

Too Much (TM) - A statement made by the viewer when he is so overwhelmed by data that he cannot report his perceptions.

Unconscious - Without awareness, sensation, or cognition.

TOM MCNEAR
2013 DAZ SMITH INTERVIEW ABOUT HIS CRV
DOCUMENT & HIS TRAINING EXPERIENCES.

Tom McNear, in 1985 you created a document of the CRV methodology, in this it also had some, what were called 'future stages' do you believe these suggestions for future stages have any merit and could be used? Did you or anyone else try or experiment with these suggestions - they seem very valid next stages for CRV, to me?

I felt that they were an appropriate "extension" of where the signal line would take us if we were willing to ride it out. Ingo and I talked about my future stages once. I asked him if he had seen them. He said, "Yes." I asked him if he agreed with them. He said (with a coy grin), "No." Actually he, with a grin, whispered, "No." That was the extent of our discussions regarding Tom's future stages. I know that Ingo felt there were more stages out there, but I don't think he truly hypnotized on or worked on what those stages would be. From my limited understanding of Ingo's last 25 years, he had several other projects he was working on, and while I know he spent time researching historical evidence that supported his existing 6 (7) stages, he didn't put a lot of effort into RV except in training a few more people along the way.

Over this last fifteen years since its public release and eighteen since the official Remote viewing program was cancelled in 1995, how do you think CRV itself has fared?

I believe that for most of the public, CRV is not on their radar screen. For most people, if you were to ask them about remote viewing, they would respond, "What's remote viewing?" For RV aficionados, RV has become a more capable and functional capability. With practice, networks of RVers are producing some amazing information that is helping Police in solving crimes and locating criminals, solving some medical/drug efficiency issues, etc. There appears to be a number of people who are providing ethical RV training and the number of practitioners and trainers is on the rise, but there is also a subset of self-serving, less than ethical people using RV to make money and a name for themselves. When the public is generally uneducated regarding RV, if their first exposure is with the "self-serving, less than ethical" side of the house, RV takes on a bad name that only serves to reinforce the notion that "this stuff doesn't work and those people are crazy." These people are doing a great disservice to RV, to science, and perhaps to mankind.

Which stage (I know you'll probably say all) do you think the student should really focus upon learning, putting in all their effort to help them learn and later use CRV?

It all begins with the ideogram. The key, to me, is ensuring you are receiving (as opposed to creating) the ideogram and then accurately expressing the "feeling motion" that accompanies it. One can glean a great deal of information just from the ideogram; throw in a powerful string of Stage 2s and you are on your way. The Stage 2s quickly build on the "feeling motion" if that "feeling motion" is appropriately felt and objectified. So I guess what I'm saying is, to me, the student should focus on the B-(feeling motion) from Stage 1 and the transition to the Stage 2s (the second half of Stage 1 and the beginning of Stage 2). Did I cheat by including half of two stages vice identifying just one?

On the subject of the ideogram, one of the finer points, I believe, is the initial ideogram or two. An untrained viewer will receive the coordinate and place "pen on paper" to capture the gestalt. If nothing happens, the viewer may feel the need to "make some kind of mark on the paper," after all, the monitor is sitting there watching and he (the monitor) expects you to do something! We don't want to disappoint the monitor do we?! It wasn't that way for me. If I didn't receive an immediate ideogram, I declared "Miss Break." I wasn't shy about doing that, I might have 2-3 Miss Breaks before making the first ideogram. I didn't mind because I knew the viewer is in charge and only the viewer can control the session. The monitor is there for the viewer and not the other way around. Ingo loved it when I was willing to declare Miss Break after Miss Break. He said that showed that I was in charge of the session and I was exerting absolute control; I wasn't there to please the monitor! Ingo often told me that session control and the ability to hold analysis in abeyance were my best strengths. Of course he trained and mentored me to be able to do so. Maybe if he and I weren't so close, I would have felt the need to "make a mark on the paper," after all, the greatest psychic in the world is sitting at the other end of the table from me and I don't want to keep him waiting... But because we were such friends, I understood what he wanted, and what he wanted was to see me exert complete control over the sessions.

After using CRV all these years, do you have any personal embellishments you've made to your process, extra stages, refinements and what not? And were you in any way intuitive before your training in CRV?

MY way is INGOs way. Strict session control! Was I intuitive before Ingo? Good question. I had nothing more than the typical déjà vu that we all have from time to time. But upon arrival at Ft Meade, before training with Ingo, we did "out bounder" sessions. My first session, to make a long story short, at the end of the session as I was bringing my perceptions back into the room, I told myself I wanted one concrete example to prove to myself that I was at the site. I saw a vivid image of a spiral staircase. When we went to the site, (Joe M. and Rob C. were my out bounders) we walked around inside the target building... no spiral staircase. Much of what I had reported was correct, but no spiral staircase. As we were getting ready to depart, I pointed to a room and asked Joe what was in that room. He stated he hadn't entered that room because a meeting was taking place at the time. I said I'd like to look in there now. We walked into the buildings "multi-purpose room;" there was a stage at one end of the room. In the middle of the stage was a spiral staircase. That was my proof. What made it even more interesting to me was that the out bounders hadn't even entered that room. They didn't see it; they didn't send me a telepathic message that the staircase was there... I was there in that room during my RV session and I saw the staircase! So, did I have abilities before Ingo, I think so, but then, don't we all?

What would you like to see for the future of CRV, where would you like to see it go and to be used? Or do you have any personal goals you would like to see CRV attain?

When Hal and Ingo started digging into RV, their goal was to "eliminate the noise" which produces inaccurate data. Ingo believed that viewers could be trained to recognize the inaccurate data (AOL). While his training went a long way toward achieving this goal, there is still a lot of work to be done. As you know, AOL can pop up any time during a session. If it comes out of the normal session sequence, it is generally incorrect, but not always. Sometimes we look back and realize it was an amazingly detailed element of the site. We believe if the AOL represents correct data, it will repeat itself and will integrate into the rest of the session, but this is an area I think needs additional work. Yes, by declaring AOL we usually clear it from the session data, but sometimes we are also "throwing out" valuable, valid data. I believe we need to somehow dig deeper and truly, truly, truly learn to identify the incorrect data. That would be an important, powerful first step. The final step would be to truly, truly, truly "eliminate the noise" so we are producing 100% pure data. That may sound impossible, and it may be, but to achieve a goal, one must first set a goal.

Do you have any last suggestions or nuggets of wisdom to share for anyone wanting to learn CRV?

Have fun. When it's no longer fun, you will stop progressing.

THE 1986 DIA CRV MANUAL

The DIA CRV manual was developed in 1986 by Paul H. Smith as the primary author, with much collaboration from the Ft. Meade Army personnel who were Ingo Swann's direct students (Bill Ray, Ed Dames, Charlene Shufelt, and Tom McNear), under the guidance of Skip Atwater, who had extensive interaction with Ingo Swann and Hal Puthoff throughout the CRV development and training process.

The manual was intended to serve as a comprehensive explanation of the theory and mechanics of CRV as developed by SRI-I. At the conclusion of the writing, Fred (Skip) Atwater forwarded a copy of the manual to Ingo Swann for his assessment. [5] This letter was his response:

"Dear Fred, Bill, Charlene, Paul, Ed and Tom. I've received and read through the material you sent along - and you've done me a great honor in taking the time to and effort to produce such a comprehensive and accurate document. I don't think I could have done this as clearly as you have and you have my deepest thanks.

If nothing else, the document at least attests to the efficacy of the training method itself. You have compiled this extremely complex technical document without the aid of written notes or taped lectures, since no materials ever left the training room and were consistently retained by myself. this point you might find suitable to point out upon occasion.

Very, very cordially,
Ingo."[4]

Public release - July 1998.

[6]The DIA CRV Manual was released into the public domain by prominent remote viewer and website owner (TKR) PJ Gaenir on July 5, 1998. (Author's note: I feel it important to include PJ's notes here as they show the context of the remote viewing community circa 1998 and the historical context of

the document).

On its release PJ had this to say about the CRV manual and why she released it:

"Before anything else, I want to say: This manual does not, and cannot, replace personal instruction in the psychic methodology of Controlled Remote Viewing. There is context and unique-to-you situations that could never be addressed in any mass-marketed form.

Those interested in obtaining CRV training from a legitimate instructor (former members of the US Gov't RV project who were Viewers and instructors in that project) may contact Paul H. Smith at RVIS or Lyn Buchanan at P>S>I for more information. I have six copies of this document on my desk. One has a simple typed cover and a copyright page. One has a "Psi-Tech" cover and a copyright page. Another two have Psi-Tech covers and no copyright page. And the other three have a large "CRV" cover with no copyright page. [Later note: OK, that's seven. Whoops!] These were sent me by an assortment of people; another dozen people offered me copies, which I didn't need. I have refused to name my sources of the manual, mostly because I feel it is irrelevant, and also because it would only be used as leverage for those who don't believe it should be public to hassle those who provided it. The original version from the military unit is the simple typed cover with the copyright page included. Whether there were previous or alternate versions within that unit, I don't know.

The legitimacy of this manual:

I am certain this is the manual written in and used in the former Army intelligence unit which utilized remote viewing. Individuals from the unit familiar with it have confirmed this either by comparing contents (page numbers/topics) with their own versions, or by glancing at it and telling me it was indeed the same document. Its accuracy concerning CRV, concerning Swann's own interpretation of CRV, its usefulness as a training document, and other issues are beyond my knowledge or comment.

The accuracy of this version of the manual:

I typed this manual in from scratch, despite that a few people had scanned copies. I wanted to be sure I learned everything in it that I might not already be aware of, and I better remember what I type. It is possible there may be typos in here somewhere. Spelling, word and hyphenation choices, were not of my doing; I copied this as faithfully as I could, and went to great effort even to format it as exactly matching the original as possible. If you find errors, please send me email and tell me so I can fix them. See also 'Changes in or notes about the online version of this manual, below.

The current state of or use of this manual:

Paul Smith *(Remote Viewing Instructional Services, Inc. [RVIS])* uses this document as a reference manual; his training manual is a gradually built notebook made up of the student's notes, essays and sessions (which is to say, RVIS doesn't really have its own training manual).

Ed Dames *(Psi-Tech Corp.)* has been using this document as a training manual for CRV since 1989 and for his "TRV" since the term first appeared in mid-1996. Caveat: I am aware that Mr. Dames now teaches "TRV," not CRV. TRV being, in his own words, "Not CRV" and "unlike anything else," is said to have "existed for 13 years" and "begins where CRV left off" and many other comments to that effect. TRV is Mr. Dames's much-publicized "invention." It has been very publicly claimed to be unique and superior to CRV, and even a great deal of insult has been heaped on instructors and students of CRV as having "inferior" methods. So, I realize that inferring Mr. Dames is really teaching CRV might cause some offense. I cannot explain the circumstance, nor can I explain why TRV as publicly released via videotape is very close to exactly like CRV, excepting some simplifications apparently added to facilitate teaching via video. This is really not my affair. I can only tell you that this CRV manual has been used as a basis of "TRV" instruction until the present time.

Lyn Buchanan *(Problems>Solutions>Innovations [P>S>I])* has developed his own CRV manual based on these methods and doesn't use this particular manual in his training, though he may use it for reference on occasion.

I don't know of any other instructors who use this. However, since all Psi-Tech students for some time have gotten a copy of it, as well as various members of the public some years ago, it is entirely possible that many "new schools of RV" are using it to one degree or another.

Changes in or notes about the online version of this manual:

(1) I included the page numbers in the table of contents, but they do not apply in this version.

(2) There is a glossary at the end of this document. The glossary contains a summary of the word definitions provided in each of the sections of the manual. For some reason not every word definition in the manual was included in the glossary. For ease of reference, I included EVERY word definition, as provided in the manual, as part of the glossary. So, that section is a bit more extensive than the original.

The six good reasons why I decided to post this manual:

1. The claims by others to have invented something which, in fact, Ingo Swann invented. Not only did he not get credit for what is rightfully his, but his own methods were taken and renamed, with some loss of quality, and then sold to an unsuspecting public. Even history was revised to make this possible. This struck me as quite unfair, both to Mr. Swann and to those interested in Remote Viewing. I thought if the original manual were available, it would be immediately obvious that certain people claiming to have invented these methods are, in fact, not telling the truth.

2. The claims by others to be using and/or teaching the CRV methods -- or a newly named derivation of them -- when in fact the later methods presented range from "not doing justice to the original" to "deeply offensive to the original form." Most seriously overcharged the general public, who really had no way of knowing the quality (or lack thereof) of what they were learning. I thought if the original manual were available, it would be immediately obvious just what has been changed, and how, and then students working on any method of RV can decide if those changes helped, harmed, or didn't matter.

3. The strongest of all of my reasons is the continuing and truly frightening cultism associated with the remote viewing field. The nature of the methods being a secret has been the primary sponsor and excuse for this to continue. The "doctrinization" of the methods has created a belief system about them being a rigid end-to-themselves. Groups and schools have, for an inordinate amount of money usually, recruited members of the public impressed by the military history of CRV, and put them in an environment which amounts to little more than cult indoctrination and has nothing whatsoever to do with any aspect of CRV which inspired the public's potential respect. I have spent quite a bit of personal time via email, telephone and in person, counseling individuals who had personal problems as a result of these various cults or simply bad training -- some from the paranoid nature of the groups, some from psyche problems caused during a creative form of 'training' better seen as hypnotic induction to bizarre belief systems, and some simply dealing with issues that badly affected their RV abilities by putting their psychology in various cognitive dissonance situations. It is more than unfair, and more than just unethical; it ought to be illegal. The only way I have to combat this dangerous seduction of the public in the name of RV is to make the supposed secrets available to the public, who should no longer have to risk their money or their sanity simply to find out what RV methods really are.

4. To allow certain facets of remote viewing history, development and methodology understanding to become more clear, not only to RV students but to the general public. Persons familiar with the developments in scientific parapsychology, for instance, will recognize that a good deal of the CRV methodology is based on the work of French researcher Rene Warcollier from the mid-1900's; it was certainly not "invented" in the 1980's. (The CRV methods are better referred to as "compiled.") Some may also recognize that many of CRV's most valuable components, such as the communication issues, are also fairly well known to parapsychologists and well educated psychics worldwide; again, most of these things were not invented in the 1980's. Ingo Swann, being insightful and accomplished in this field, recognized the value of many different sources and combined them in his methods; this combination of sources is one of the strengths of his methods. Not everybody is aware of this though, and others who deserve credit are often overlooked in the assumption that Swann invented it all. There are two main results of this understanding: the first being to un-guru-ize Mr. Swann, who is a brilliant and dedicated psychic, author and researcher who never asked to be made into a stone icon by the world at large for this; there are a long list of reasons to respect him without projecting things he is not responsible for upon him. Also, hopefully, to un-guru-ize other persons who may be teaching these methods, which should help with reason #3 above. The second result is the realization that, since many of the most useful aspects of CRV are known to others and have in fact been known for longer periods than CRV itself has existed, then these methods, albeit very useful, cannot claim sole expertise or sole competence when it comes to successful psi work. The supposed superiority of anybody trained in RV methods, vs. "natural psychics," is a marketing and ego myth and nothing more.

5. I feel that remote viewing--particularly what it can be used for, with what success, and the value of methods training--has been grossly misrepresented in the media. Remote Viewing itself has very pronounced limitations. To the public who knows nothing of the "technology," it sounds cosmic, and one is forced to pay large sums of money to learn the secret methods just to figure out what is actually involved -- almost invariably with no evidence whatsoever of the value of the methods prior to paying for them. (In fact, the main advertisements for RV are the notable accomplishment of a current remote viewer [Joseph W. McMoneagle] who does not even USE these methods.) I think after reading this manual people will realize that CRV / TRV / all the other RVs are, first and foremost, just somebody's way of going about being psychic.

No method has even half the inferred accuracy, sureness, or cosmic clarity that various RV methods have been advertised as having. I happen to have respect for CRV, but I realize it is just one path of many. As a side note, this manual will also make clear the humorous ostentatiousness of the presentation of these methods: "facilitate a movement exercise" means, in effect, someone told you to look some distance to the left. "Iterate the coordinates and acquire the signal line while remaining in structure" translates to something like, 'monitor says the target #, viewer tunes in and writes down his impressions on the right side of the paper.' It really is comical once you understand CRV, to hear certain individuals in the media talking about RV methodologies, making them sound so incredibly complicated and high-tech; it is a sales pitch, used to obscure, not clarify. Personally I think remote viewing can only benefit from taking this sort of mystery out of the methods.

6. The last--but a very small--reason I'm putting this manual online has to do with my own personal involvement with CRV methodologies and remote viewing. I have invested a good 60+ hours per week into RV-related work for nearly three years, mostly email communication with the public, most to support CRV and support its instructors. I have maintained the privacy of the methods, giving only "tips and tidbits." I have avoided training others because I made the commitment not to.

Over the course of these years I have directed well over $100,000 in training monies to CRV instructors, directly or indirectly via my online enterprises of various kinds, as well as providing them support in other ways. In return for this, I have been offered and paid the commission of zero. At this point, I feel I have more than "paid my dues." So, guilt at taking potential students away from qualified CRV instructors isn't bothering me. I believe serious students will recognize the need for personal training. Everybody else, or those without the funds, probably wouldn't have bought it anyway. As a second part to the personal section, I feel I have spent nearly three years "defending" remote viewing from charlatans, cynics, and dis/misinformation both organized and chaotic. As I am 'retiring' I am not going to be around to defend RV anymore; to provide an alternative to some of the bizarre media hype, to provide references to real viewers and scientists, etc.; so in a small way, this manual is my effort to help stop the BS that is choking the remote viewing field once and for all. Hopefully it can accomplish what I could not: getting down to earth facts to the public, without money, without cults, without nonsense. Considering the first five reasons above, I no longer feel a sense of moral reluctance to publish the CRV manual. For the good of the world, the public, and remote viewing itself, these methods need to be put into the public domain. (I will not, however, publish the other manuals or items used by CRV instructors without their express permission.) Since I am retiring from "online RV" at this time (4 July 1998) to free up time to pursue my own RV work, I felt posting this manual would be the one last gift I could provide to the public. It may not help in the sense of methods training, but it ought to help in the sense of dealing with the five reasons listed above, and they are very good reasons for making it available.

It's long overdue.

My own view on the manual:

Though I support CRV, I do not necessarily agree with all aspects of CRV, particularly the manner some are presented in this manual (this most clear in the issues related to monitoring). In my view, there is a certain lack of context, and a perspective that demonstrates its writing by a student rather than an experienced instructor. The manual may accurately represent what the authors were taught, but I am not sure it is the same thing that the instructor would have written, and over time my own perspective on "the approach" within the methods has shifted. I have learned various degrees of various people's versions of various RV methodologies, and like everybody who has given psi any real thought, have come to my own conclusions. What works for me is what I use, and CRV is a part of that, but certainly not the sole or final answer.

I initially had put footnotes in this manual, to help clarify things. But eventually I realized that in some cases I simply had to disagree with some statement, or something else that in some way seemed to detract from it. Then I decided, if I have something to say, I have my own forums for doing so; there is no reason to invade the sanctity of a historical document with my opinions. And if the manual, sans the footnotes, is totally opaque to most non-methods people and leaves them more confused than when they began -- well, that's just the way it goes. Take it up with the guy who wrote it!

Copyright issues:

The copyright of this document is attributed to Ingo Swann. Ingo however denies any credit for, participation in, or responsibility toward the document or its copyright. I called him and asked if I could post it. He said it wasn't his and he didn't care. It was written by Paul H. Smith. Paul however wrote it as a work for hire while employed by the DOD/DIA. The DIA did not classify the document, which in legal terms puts it in the public domain (the gov't cannot copyright, they can only classify; unclassified materials are public record; nobody else can then claim ownership of what began a gov't document). SRI-I might lay claim to it, as they funded Swann to develop the proprietary methods in it. But at this point, copies of the document have been disseminated publicly since 1989, which not only would invalidate any SRI/DIA copyright claim (since they have never prosecuted for copyright thus far), but in that case, they'd have to start with the main distributor, which would be Psi-Tech Corp. According to Smith, since the document was a DIA document but not classified, it has been public record (despite that the public hasn't before had open access to it) since it was written. It was written and dated 1986. So, as far as I'm concerned, it is mine to publish if I please. I realize that this copy

114

will immediately be stolen off the WWW by others, stripped of all relevant notes, and published elsewhere. That is unfortunate, but there is nothing I can do about that. I considered putting it in a locked .pdf file, but felt that might limit public access to it. I have always made a point to make my projects available to the public without charge and as accessible as possible... I didn't want this to be an exception. For those of you making links to the document, please be kind enough to your visitors to link to the version on my Firedocs site, which is the most 'official' copy possible at this point.

Or, at least have the courtesy to include Mr. Swann's own notes with your copy.

Thanks."
Palyne "PJ" Gaenir

Firedocs Remote Viewing Collection.
http://www.firedocs.com/remoteviewing/

INTRODUCTION TO THE DIA CRV MANUAL
BY PAUL H. SMITH [MAJOR, RET] 1998.

For a number of what I consider to be very good reasons, I strenuously resisted making the DIA CRV manual public. Since some of my former colleagues had fewer reservations about its dissemination, it now appears inevitable that the manual will become widely available, beginning with its posting here on this webpage. The best I can do now, it would seem, is to at least provide its context so people will better know how to take it.

In 1983-1984, six personnel from the military remote viewing unit at Ft. Meade participated in training contracted from SRI-International. This was the recently-developed coordinate remote viewing training, and the primary developer and trainer was the legendary Ingo Swann. One of the first trainees,

Rob Cowart, was diagnosed with cancer, and was medically retired from active duty, terminating his training after only a few months. (Sadly Rob, who had been in remission for many years, died a year or so ago from the disease.) The second, Tom "Nance" (his pseudonym in Jim Schnabel's book, Remote Viewers) completed all training through Stage VI as the proof-of-principle "guinea pig." His results were not just impressive. Some could even be considered spectacular.

Beginning in January of 1984, the remaining four of us began training with Ingo in California and New York. This contract lasted for a full year. Ed Dames, "Liam," Charlene, and myself continued through until December (though Ed dropped out just before completion due to the birth of a son). We completed through Stage III training with Ingo. Towards the end of 1984 our patron and commander, Major General Burt Stubblebine was forced to retire and the RV program was threatened with termination. Consequently, no further contracts were let for training.

During the course of 1985, our future was very uncertain. However, the branch chief, together with Fred "Skip" Atwater (the training and operations officer), were hopeful that the unit would find a sponsor (which indeed happened) and decided to continue our training through Stage VI, with the help of Nance's experience and considerable documentation and theoretical understanding that Atwater and others had managed to accrue.

At the conclusion of our training, and with a number of successful operational and training projects under

117

our belts to show that CRV really did work, the further decision was made to try and capture in as pure a form as possible the Ingo methodology. The reasoning was that we might never get any more out-of-house training approved, yet we needed to be able to perpetuate the methodology even after the folks with the "institutional memory" eventually left the unit. I had developed the reputation of being the "word man" in the unit, plus Skip and the branch chief seemed to think I had a firm understanding and grasp of the theory and methodology, so I was asked to write a manual capturing as much of the CRV methodology as possible, with the assistance of the others who had been trained.

We pooled our notes, and I wrote each section, then ran it by the others for their suggestions and comments. Corrections and suggestions were evaluated and added if it could be established that they matched true "Ingo theory." Skip and Tom both reviewed the manuscript and provided their input as well. When the thing was finally done, a copy was forwarded to Ingo, who deemed it a "comprehensive and accurate document." Finally, Skip provided a three-page introductory section which it now turns out was apparently originally drafted by Joe McMoneagle. The finished version was printed at the DIA press in May 1986. It was a specialty run, and was never given an official DIA document number. I don't believe any more than thirty or so were printed.

Things to keep in mind about the CRV manual:

It wasn't intended as a training manual per se, and

certainly not as a standalone training manual. It's primary purpose was to capture and preserve for posterity Ingo's methodology. The very first page declares that it was "prepared to serve as a comprehensive explanation of the theory and mechanics" of CRV, and as a "guide for future training programs." We certainly didn't develop it as a "how to." Since we always assumed any further training to be done would either involve Ingo or someone who had already been trained, the manual did not incorporate lessons-learned, nor the practical implementation of CRV in an operational setting, nor even to explain how one taught people to do CRV, nor why CRV included certain points of theory and process in its methodological base. There are of course lots of things to be said about all these points, and we had ambitions at one time of writing a practical hands-on RV training manual. Unfortunately, events conspired against us and it never happened.

In the hands of someone who understands CRV and already knows what is going on, the manual can be extremely useful in teaching others to remote view. We used it in the theory and lecture part of the CRV training of everyone who became a CRVer at the Ft. Meade unit (the one exception was Lyn Buchanan, whom we taught CRV before the manual became reality). I have used it exclusively in my commercial training activities (augmented, of course, by my own experience in training and operations), and I think most, if not all of my students would confirm the efficacy of this approach. It represents CRV in its purest form, and any departures from the principles it contains should be examined at long and hard before they are accepted. There are already a number of alleged "product improvements" based upon the CRV manual that not only are not improvements, but if they aren't just changing "happy" to "glad" or adding superfluous embellishments, may even be outright eviscerations of CRV's principles and effective methodologies. In considering these "new versions" of CRV methodology, it is definitely a case of caveat emptor.

I see as a positive benefit of posting the manual that some of the chicanery and foolishness may finally be unveiled that has been able to persist around derivatives of CRV because the "bottom line" hasn't until now been available. There are of course those who will offer as their excuse that this manual represents obsolete technology. My response is that none of its derivatives have thus far demonstrated anything better--or in most cases even as good-- under similar constraints.

Paul H. Smith
Austin, TX
3 July 1998

THE 1986 DIA CRV MANUAL

INTRODUCTION

A. General:

The following definitions and descriptions are provided to acquaint the reader with the remote viewing phenomenon and a typical remote viewing session.

1. Definitions:

a. Remote Viewing (RV): The name of a method of psychoenergetic perception. A term coined by SRI-International and defined as "the acquisition and description, by mental means, of information blocked from ordinary perception by distance, shielding, or time."

b. Coordinate Remote Viewing (CRV): The process of remote viewing using geographic coordinates for cueing or prompting.

c. Remote Viewer: Often referred to in the text simply as "viewer", the remote viewer is a person who employs his mental faculties to perceive and obtain information to which he has no other access and of which he has no previous knowledge concerning persons, places, events, or objects separated from him by time, distance, or other intervening obstacles.

d. Monitor: The individual who assists the viewer in a remote viewing session. The monitor provides the coordinate, observes the viewer to help insure he stays in proper structure (discussed below), records relevant session information, provides appropriate feedback when required, and provides objective analytic support to the viewer as necessary. The monitor plays an especially important role in training beginning viewers.

2. Descriptions:

a. Remote Viewing Session: In a remote viewing session an individual or "viewer" attempts to acquire and describe by mental means alone information about a designated site. The viewer is not told what the site is that must be described but is provided a cue or prompt which designates the site.

b. Session Dynamics: In conducting a coordinate remote viewing session, a remote viewer and a monitor begin by seating themselves at the opposite ends of a table in a special remote viewing room equipped with paper and pens, a tape recorder, and a TV camera which allows either recording for documentation, or monitoring by individuals outside the room. The room is homogeneously colored, acoustically tiled, and featureless, with light controlled by a dimmer, so that environmental distractions can be minimized. The session begins when the monitor provides cueing or prompting information (geographic coordinates in this case) to the remote viewer. The remote viewer is given no additional identifying information, and at this point has no conscious knowledge of the actual site. For training purposes, the monitor is allowed to know enough about the site to enable him to determine when accurate versus inaccurate information is being provided.

The session then proceeds with the monitor repeating the prompting information at appropriate intervals and providing necessary feedback. The remote viewer generates verbal responses and sketches, until a coherent response to the overall task requirement emerges.

c. Post Session Dynamics: After the session is over, the remote viewer and monitor obtain specific information about the site in picture/descriptive form. The remote viewer and monitor then discuss the session results.

B. Background:

In early 1980, an SRI - International (SRI-I) subcontractor developed a training procedure known as Coordinate Remote Viewing to satisfy R&D demands on SRI-I to enhance the reliability (scientific replicability) of remote viewing (RV). The subcontractor's approach to improving the reliability of RV was to focus on the control of those factors that in his view tend to introduce "noise" into the RV product (imaginative, environmental, and interviewer overlays). The basic components of this training procedure consist of:

(1) Repeated site address (geographic coordinate) presentation, with quick reaction response by the remote viewer; coupled with a restrictive format for reporting perceived information (to minimize imaginative overlays).
(2) The use of a specially designed, acoustically tiled, relatively featureless, homogeneously colored "viewing chamber" (to minimize environmental overlays).

(3) The adoption of a strictly prescribed, limited interviewer patter (to minimize interviewer overlays).

The training procedure requires that the trainee learn a progressive, multi-stage acquisition process postulated to correspond to increased contact with the site.

At present there are six "stages" of training. In general, these stages progress as follows:

(1) "**Stage I**" sites (islands, mountains, deserts, etc.).

(2) "**Stage II**" sites (sites of quality sensory value— sites which are uniquely describable through touch, taste, sound, color, or odor—such as glaciers, volcanoes, industrial plants, etc.) .

(3) "**Stage III**" sites (sites possessing significant dimensional characteristics such as buildings, bridges,

airfields, etc.) .

(4) "**Stage IV**" sites for which the trainee begins to form qualitative mental precepts (technical area, military feeling, research, etc.).

(5) "**Stage V**" sites for which the trainee learns to "interrogate" qualitative mental precepts in an attempt to produce analytical target descriptions (aircraft tracking radar, biomedical research facility, tank production plant, etc.).

(6) "**Stage VI**" sites which involve the trainee in direct, three-dimensional assessment and modeling of the site and/or the relationship of site elements to one another (airplanes inside one of three camouflaged hangars or a military compound with a command building, barracks, motor pool, and underground weapons storage area).

The following document has been prepared to serve as a comprehensive explanation of the theory and mechanics of CRV as developed by SRI-I. It is intended for individuals who have no in-depth understanding of the technology and as a guide for future training programs. Particular attention should be paid to the glossary at the end of the document and to the terms as defined in the text, as they are the only acceptable definitions to be used when addressing the methodology presented.

THEORY

A. Concept:

As will be explained in greater detail below, remote viewing theory postulates a non-material "Matrix" in which any and all information about any person, place or thing may be obtained through the agency of a hypothesized "signal line." The viewer psychically perceives and decodes this signal line and objectifies the information so obtained.

A remote viewing session consists of both the interaction of a remote viewer with the signal line, and the interaction between the viewer and the monitor. The monitor and viewer are generally seated at opposite ends of a table. The viewer has a pen and plenty of paper in front of him. The monitor observes the viewer, and determines when the viewer is ready to begin. When the viewer places his pen on the left side of the paper in preparation to record the coordinate. The monitor then reads the coordinate, the viewer writes it, and the session proceeds from that point according to theory and methodology as discussed at length below.

B. Definitions:

1. Matrix: Something within which something else originates or takes form or develops. A place or point of origin or growth.

2. Signal: Something that incites into action; an immediate cause or impulse. In radio propagation theory, the carrier wave that is received by the radio or radar receiving set.

3. Signal Line: The hypothesized train of signals emanating from the Matrix (discussed below) and perceived by the remote viewer, which transports the

information obtained through the remote viewing process.

4. Wave: A disturbance or variation that transfers itself and energy progressively from point to point in a medium or in space in such a way that each particle or element influences the adjacent ones and that may be in the form of an elastic deformation or of a variation of level or pressure, of electric or magnetic intensity, of electric potential, or of temperature.

5. Aperture: An opening or open space; hole, gap, cleft, chasm, slit. In radar, the electronic gate that controls the width and dispersion pattern of the radiating signal or wave.

6. Gestalt: A unified whole; a configuration, pattern, or organized field having specific properties that cannot be derived from the summation of its component parts.

7. Evoking: (Evoke: "to call forth or up; to summon; to call forth a response; elicit".) Iteration of the coordinate or alternate prompting method is the mechanism which "evokes" the signal line, calling it up, causing it to impinge on the autonomic nervous system and unconsciousness for transmittal through the viewer and on to objectification (discussed at length in STRUCTURE).

8. Coding/Encoding/Decoding: The information conveyed on the signal line is translated into an informational system (a code) allowing data to be "transmitted" by the signal line. Upon receiving the signal, the viewer must "decode" this information through proper structure to make it accessible. This

concept is very similar to radio propagation theory, in which the main carrier signal is modulated to convey the desired information.

C. Discussion:

The Matrix has been described as a huge, non-material, highly structured, mentally accessible "framework" of information containing all data, and pertaining to everything in both the physical and non-physical universe. In the same vein as Jung's Cosmic Unconsciousness, the matrix is open to and comprises all conscious entities as well as information relating to everything else living or nonliving by accepted human definition. It is this informational framework from which the data encoded on the signal line originates. This Matrix can be envisioned as a vast, three-dimensional geometric arrangement of dots, each dot representing a discrete information bit. Each geographic location on the earth has a corresponding segment of the Matrix corresponding exactly to the nature of the physical location. When the viewer is prompted by the coordinate or other targeting methodology, he accesses the signal line for data derived from the Matrix. By successfully acquiring (detecting) this information from the signal line, then coherently decoding it through his conscious awareness and faculties, he makes it available for analysis and further exploitation by himself or others.

Remote viewing is made possible through the agency of a hypothetical "signal line." In a manner roughly analogous to standard radio propagation theory, this signal line is a carrier wave which is inductively modulated by its intercourse with information, and may be detected and decoded by a remote viewer. The signal line radiates in many different frequencies, and its impact on the viewer's perceptive faculties is controlled through a phenomenon known as "aperture".

Essentially, when the remote viewer first detects the signal line in Stage I* it manifests itself as a sharp, rapid influx of signal energy--representing large gestalts of information. In this situation, we therefore speak of a "narrow" aperture, since only a very narrow portion of the signal line is allowed to access the consciousness. In later stages involving longer, slower, more enduring waves, the aperture is spoken of as being "wider."

*NOTE: For the sake of clarity, ease of instruction, and facility of control, RV methodology is divided into discreet, progressive "stages", each dealing with different or more detailed aspects of the site. Stage I is the first and most general of the six stages thus far identified. Each stage is a natural progression, building on the information obtained during the previous stage. Each session must start with Stage I, progress on through Stage II, Stage III, and so forth, through the highest stage to be completed in that particular session.

D. Levels of Consciousness:

1. Definitions:

a. **Subconscious:** Existing in the mind but not immediately available to consciousness; affecting thought, feeling, and behavior without entering awareness. The mental activities just below the threshold of consciousness.

b. **Subliminal:** Existing or functioning outside the area of conscious awareness; influencing thought, feeling, or behavior in a manner unperceived by personal or subjective consciousness; designed to influence the mind on levels other than that of conscious awareness and especially by presentation too brief to be consciously perceived.

c **Limen:** The threshold of consciousness; the interface between the subconscious and conscious.

d. **Liminal:** At the limen; verging on consciousness.

e. **Supraliminal:** Above the limen; in the realm of conscious awareness.

f. **Conscious:** Perceiving apprehending, or noticing with a degree of controlled thought or observation; recognizing as existent, factual, or true. Recognizing as factual or existent something external. Present especially to the senses. Involving rational power, perception, and awareness. By definition, the "conscious" part of the human being is that portion of the human consciousness which is linked most closely to and limited by the material world.

g. **Autonomic Nervous system (ANS):** A part of the vertebrate nervous system that innervates smooth and cardiac muscle and glandular tissues, governs actions that are more or less automatic, and consists of the sympathetic nervous system and the parasympathetic nervous system (Webster's 3rd Int. Unabr.).

h. **Ideogram (I):** The reflexive mark made on the paper as a result of the impingement of the signal on

130

the autonomic nervous system and its subsequent transmittal through this system to the arm and hand muscles, which transfers it through the pen onto the paper.

i **Analytic Overlay (AOL):** Conscious subjective interpretation of signal line data, which may or may not be relevant to the site. *(Discussed at length in STRUCTURE.)*

j. **Automatic vs. Autonomic:** Reception and movement of the signal line information through the viewer's system** and into objectification is an autonomic process as opposed to an automatic one, which itself implies an action arising and subsiding entirely within the system rather than from without.

**NOTE: When the word "system" is used without qualifiers such as "autonomic", etc., it refers in a general sense to all the integrated and integrative biological (and perhaps metaphysical as well) elements and components of the viewer himself which enable him to function in this mode known as "remote viewing".

2. Discussion:

RV theory relies on a rather Freudian model of human consciousness levels. The lowest level of consciousness is paradoxically named the "unconscious". All this label really means is that that part of our mental processes we know as physical "awareness" or "consciousness" does not have access to what goes on there. It is apparently this part of the individuals psyche that first detects and receives the signal line. From here it is passed to the autonomic nervous system. When the signal line impinges on the ANS, the information is converted into a reflexive nervous response conducted through muscular channels controlled by the ANS. If so allowed, this response will manifest itself as an ideogram. At the same time, the signal is passed up through the subconscious, across the limen, and into the lower fringes of the consciousness. This is the highest state of consciousness from the standpoint of human material awareness. However, the normal waking consciousness poses certain problems for remote viewing, occasioned largely because of the linear, analytic thought processes which are societally enhanced and ingrained from our earliest stages of cognitive development. While extremely useful in a society relying heavily on quantitative data and technological development, such analytic thinking hampers remote viewing by the manufacture of what is known as "analytic overlay", or AOL.

As the signal line surges up across the limen and into the threshold areas of consciousness, the mind's conscious analytic process feels duty bound to assign coherence to what at first blush seems virtually incomprehensible data coming from an unaccustomed source. It must in other words make a "logical" assessment based on the impressions being received. Essentially, the mind jumps to one or a number of instantaneous conclusions about the incoming information without waiting for sufficient information to make an accurate judgment. This process is completely reflexive, and happens even when not desired, by the individual involved. Instead of allowing holistic "right brain" processes (through which the signal line apparently manifests itself) to assemble a complete and accurate concept, untrained "left brain" based analytic processes seize upon whatever bit of information seems most familiar and forms an AOL construct based on it.

For example, a viewer has been given the coordinates to a large, steel girder bridge. A flash of a complex, metal, manmade structure may impinge on the liminary regions of the viewer's mind, but so briefly that no coherent response can be made to it. The conscious mind, working at a much greater speed than the viewer expects, perceives bits and pieces such as angles, riveted girders, and a sense of being "roofed over" and paved, whereupon it suggests to the physical awareness of the viewer that the site is the outside of a large sports stadium. The "image" is of course wrong, but is at least composed of factual elements, though these have been combined by the viewer's overeager analytical processes to form an erroneous conclusion.

E. Learning Theory:

1. Definitions:

a. Overtraining: The state reached when the individual's learning system is over saturated and is "burned out", analogous to a muscle that has been overworked and can no longer extend or contract until it is allowed to rest and rebuild fibers that have been broken down by the stress, or reinforce those that have been newly acquired by new demands placed upon the muscle.

b. Absorption: Assimilation, as by incorporation or by the digestive process.

c. Cognitron: A cognitron is an assemblage of neurons, linked together by interconnecting synapses, and which when stimulated by the mind's recall system produce a composite concept of their various subparts. Each neuron is charged with an element of the overall concept, which when combined with the elements of its fellow neurons produces the final concept which the cognitron represents. As a human learns new facts, skills or behaviors, neurons are connecting into new cognitrons, the connecting synapses of which are more and more reinforced with use.

d. Neuron: "A nerve cell with all its processes." The apparent fundamental physical building block of mental and nervous processes. Neurons are the basic element in the formation of cognitrons, and may be linked into varying configurations by the formation or rearrangement of synapse chains.

e. Synapse: The interstices between neurons over which nerve impulses must travel to carry information from the senses, organs, and muscles to the brain and back, and to conduct mental processes.

f. Learning Curve: The graphic representation of the standard success-to-session ratio of a remote viewer trainee. The typical curve demonstrates high success for the first one to a few attempts, a sudden and drastic drop in success, then a gradual improvement curve until a relatively high plateau is reached.

g. "First-Time" Effect: In any human activity or skill a phenomenon exists known as "beginner's luck." In remote viewing, this phenomenon is manifest as especially successful performance at the first attempt at psychic functioning, after which the success rate drops sharply, to be built up again gradually through further training. This effect is hypothesized to result from the initial excitation of hereditary but dormant psi conducting neuronal channels which, when first stimulated by attempted psychoenergetic functioning "catch the analytic system off guard, as it were, allowing high-grade functioning with little other system interference. Once the initial novelty wears off, the analytic systems which have been trained for years to screen all mental functions attempt to account for and control the newly awakened neural pathways, thereby generating increasing amounts of masking "mental noise", or AOL.

h. Noise: The effect of the various types of overlay, innervates, etc. that serve to obscure or confuse the viewer's reception and accurate decoding of the signal line. Noise must be dealt with properly and in structure to allow the viewer to accurately recognize the difference between a valid signal and his own incorrect internal processes.

2. Discussion:

Learning theory for RV methodology is governed by the idea that the student should "quit on a high point." Traditionally, the learning of a skill concentrates on rote repetition, reiterating the skill a large number of times until it is consistently performed correctly. Recent developments in learning theory which have been applied with particular success in sports training methodology indicate that the rote repetition concept tends more to reinforce incorrect performance as opposed to developing the proper behavior or skill. Much success has been realized by implementing the concept of "quitting on a high point." That is, when a skill or behavior has been executed correctly, taking an extended break from the training at that point allows the learning processes to "remember" the correct behavior by strengthening the neurological relays that have been established in the brain by the correct procedure.

The phenomenon of overtraining is a very real danger in the training cycle generally brought about by pushing ahead with training until the learning system of the viewer is totally saturated and cannot absorb anymore. This results in system collapse, which in effect is a total failure to function psychically at all. To avoid this, the normal practice has been to work an appropriate number of sessions a day (anywhere from one to several, depending on each individual trainee's capacity and level of training and experience) for a set number of days or weeks (also individually dependent), with a lay off period between training periods to allow time for assimilation or "absorption." Even with this precaution, overtraining can sometimes strike, and the only remedy becomes a total training layoff, then a gradual reintroduction.

It is extremely important that the viewer inform the monitor when he is feeling especially good about his performance in remote viewing training, so that a training break may be initiated on this high point. To continue to push beyond this threatens a slide into overtraining. It is very important that should the viewer in the course of the training session become aware that he has experienced some important "cognition" or understanding, or if the monitor perceives that this is the case, the session must here also be halted. This allows time both for this cognition to be fully matriculated into the viewer's system and for the accompanying elation of discovery to dissipate.

The fact that CRV methodology is arranged into six distinct stages implies that there is a learning progression from one stage to the next. To determine when a student viewer is ready to advance to the next stage, certain milestones are looked for. Though the peculiarities of each stage make certain of these criteria relevant only to that specific stage, general rules may still be outlined. When a viewer has consistently demonstrated control and replication of all pertinent stage elements and has operated "noise free" (i.e., properly handling AOL and other system distractions in structure) for five or six sessions, he is ready to write a stage summation essay and move on to the introductory lectures for the next stage. Essay writing is an important part of the CRV training, and serves as a sort of intellectual "objectification" of the material learned. Through student essays the instructor is able to determine how thoroughly and accurately the student has internalized the concepts taught.

F. Reference material:

1. Theory:
   a: Dixon, Norman, Preconscious Processing, New York: Wiley, 1981.

2. Learning Theory:
   a. Fukushima, K. and Miyake, S., "A Self-organizing Neural Network with a Function of Associative memory: Feed-back Type Cognition", Biological Cybernetics, 28

(1978), pp. 201-208.

b. Fukushima, K. "Neocognitron: A Self-organizing Neural Network Model for a Mechanism of Pattern Recognition Unaffected by Shift in Position," Biological Cybernetics, 36 (1980), pp. 197-202.

c. Linn, Louis, "The Discriminating Function of the Ego, Psychoanalytic Quarterly, 23 (1954), pp. 38-47.

d. Shevrin, H., and Dickman, Scott, "The Psychological Unconscious: A Necessary Assumption for All Psychological Theory?" American Psychologist, vol. 35, no. 5 (May 1980), pp. 421-434.

e. Westlake, P. R., "The Possibilities of Neural Holographic Processes within the Brain," Kybernetic, vol. 7, no. 4, pp. 129-153.

STRUCTURE

A. Concept:

"Structure" is a singularly important element in remote viewing theory. The word "structure" signifies the orderly process of proceeding from general to specific in accessing the signal line, of objectifying in proper sequence all data bits and RV related subjective phenomena (i.e., see aesthetic impact as discussed in STAGE III), and rigorous extraction of AOL from the viewer's system by conscientious objectification. Structure is executed in a formal ordered format sequence using pen and paper. A sample format will be provided as each stage is discussed in turn, since different elements are used in each.

B. Definitions and Discussion:

1. Inclemencies:

Personal considerations that might degrade or even preclude psychic functioning--muscle pains, colds, allergies, menstrual cramps, hangovers, mental and emotional stress, etc., could cause increased difficulty to the viewer in accessing the signal line, but could be "worked through", and ultimately are only minor nuisances.

Only hunger and a pressing need to eliminate body wastes cause the system to totally not function. It is important, though, that the viewer identify and declare any inclemencies either at the first of the session or as they are recognized, since unattended agendas such as these can color or distort the viewer's functioning if not eliminated from the system through objectification (see below). Preferably, the monitor will ask the viewer if he has any personal inclemencies even before the first iteration of the coordinate so as to purge the system as much as possible before beginning the session proper.

There is evidence that an additional category of inclemencies exist, which we might refer to as environmental inclemencies. Extremely low frequency (ELF) electromagnetic radiation may have a major role in this. Experience and certain research suggests that changes in the Earth's geomagnetic field--normally brought about by solar storms, or "sunspots", may degrade the remote viewer's system, or actually cause it to cease functioning effectively altogether. Ongoing research projects are attempting to discover the true relationship, if any, between solar storms, ELF, and human psychic functioning.

2. Objectification:

The act of physically saying out loud and writing down information. In this methodology, objectification serves several important functions. First, it allows the information derived from the signal line to be recorded and expelled from the system, freeing the viewer to receive further information and become better in tune with the signal line. Secondly, it makes the system independently aware that its contributions have been acknowledged and recorded. Thirdly, it allows re-input of the information into the system as necessary for further prompting. In effect, objectification "gives reality" to the signal line and the information it conveys. Finally, objectification allows non-signal line derived material (inclemencies, AOLS, etc.,) that might otherwise clutter the system and mask valid signal line data to be expelled.

3. I/A/B Sequence:

The core of all CRV structure, the "I/A/B" sequence is the fundamental element of Stage I, which is itself in turn the foundation for site acquisition and further site detection and decoding in subsequent CRV stages. The sequence is composed of an ideogram (the "I"), which is a spontaneous graphic representation of the sites major gestalt; the "A" component or "feeling/motion" involved in the ideogram; and the "B" component, or first analytic response to the signal line. (A full discussion may be found in the Stage I section below.)

4. Feedback:

Those responses provided during the session to the viewer to indicate if he has detected and properly decoded site relevant information; or, information provided at some point after completion of the RV session or project to "close the loop" as it were, providing the viewer with closure as to the site accessed and allowing him to assess the quality of his performance more accurately.

In-session feedback, with which we will be here most concerned, is usually only used extensively in earlier stages of the training process, and has several interconnected functions. The very nature of the RV phenomena makes it often only rather tenuously accessible to one's physically based perceptions, and therefore difficult to recognize. Feedback is provided after correct responses to enable the viewer to immediately identify those perceptions which produced the correct response and associate them

141

with proper psychic behavior. Secondly, it serves to develop much needed viewer confidence by immediately rewarding the viewer and letting him know that he is being successful. Finally, it helps keep the viewer on the proper course and connected with the signal line, preventing him from falling into AOL drive and wandering off on a tangent.

a. **Correct (abbreviated "C"):**   The data bit presented by the trainee viewer is assessed by the monitor to be a true component of the site.

b. **Probably Correct (PC):** Data presented cannot be fully assessed by the monitor as being accurate site information, but it would be reasonable to assume because of its nature that the information is valid for the site.

c. **Near Site (N):** Data objectified by the viewer are elements of objects or locations near the site.

d. **Can't Feed Back (CFB):**   monitor has insufficient feedback information to evaluate data produced by the viewer.

e. **Site (S):** Tells the former that he has successfully acquired and debriefed the site.   In elementary training sessions, this usually signifies the termination of the session.   At later stages, when further information remains to be derived from the site, the session may continue on beyond full acquisition of the site.

f. **Silence:** When information objectified by the trainee viewer is patently incorrect, the monitor simply remains silent, which the viewer may freely

interpret as an incorrect
response.

In line with the learning theory upon which this
system is based, the intent is to avoid reinforcing any
negative behavior or response. Therefore, there is
no feedback for an incorrect response; and any other
feedback information is strictly limited to those as
defined above.

It should be noted here that the above refers to
earlier stages of the training process. Later stages do
away with in-session feedback to the viewer, and at
even later stages the monitor himself is denied access
to any site information or feedback until the session
is over.

5. Self-Correcting Characteristic:

The tendency of the ideogram to re-present itself if
improperly or incompletely decoded. If at the
iteration of the coordinate an ideogram is produced
and then decoded with the wrong "A" & "B"
components, or not completely decoded, upon the
next iteration of the coordinate the same ideogram
will appear, thereby informing the viewer that he has
made an error somewhere in the procedure. On rare
occasions, the ideogram will be re-presented even
when   it   has   been   properly   decoded.

This almost inevitably occurs if the site is extremely
uniform, such as the middle of an ocean, a sandy
desert, glacier, etc., where nothing else but one single
aspect is present.

6. AOL ("Analytic Overlay"):

The analytic response of the viewer's mind to signal

line input. An AOL is usually wrong, especially in early stages, but often does possess valid elements of the site that are contained in the signal line; hence, a light house may produce an AOL of "factory chimney" because of its tall, cylindrical shape. AOLs may be recognized in several ways. First, if there is a comparator present ("it looks like...", "it's sort of...", etc.) the information present will almost inevitably be an AOL, and should always be treated as one. Secondly, a mental image that is sharp, clear, and static--that is, there is no motion present in it, and in fact it appears virtually to be a mental photograph of the site--is also certainly AOL.   Hesitation in production of the "B" component in Stage I coordinate remote viewing, or a response that is out of structure anywhere in the system are also generally sure indicators that AOL is present.   Finally, the monitor or viewer can frequently detect AOL by the inflection of the viewer's voice or other micro behaviors. Data delivered as a question rather than a statement should be recognized as usually being AOL.

AOLs are dealt with by declaring/objectifying them as soon as they are recognized, and writing "AOL Break" on the right side of the paper, then writing a brief description of the AOL immediately under that. This serves to acknowledge to the viewer's system that the AOL has been recognized and duly recorded and that it is not what is desired, thereby purging the system of unwanted noise and debris and allowing the signal line in its purity to be acquired and decoded properly.

7. Breaks:
The mechanism developed to allow the system*** to

144

be put on "hold", providing the opportunity to flush out AOLS, deal with temporary inclemencies, or make system adjustments, allowing a fresh start with new momentum. There are seven types of breaks:

NOTE: When the word "system" is used without qualifiers such as "autonomic", etc., it refers in a general sense to all the integrated and integrative biological (and perhaps metaphysical as well) elements and components of the viewer himself which enable him to function in this mode known as "remote viewing".

a. AOL Break: As mentioned above, allows the signal line to be put on hold while AOL is expelled from the system.

b. Confusion Break (often "Conf Bk"): When the viewer becomes confused by events in his environment or information in the signal line to the degree that impressions he is receiving are hopelessly entangled, a Confusion Break is called. Whatever time necessary is allowed for the confusion to dissipate, and when necessary the cause for confusion is declared much like it is done with AOL. The RV process is then resumed with an iteration of the coordinate.

c. Too Much Break ("TM Break"): When too much information is provided by the signal line all at once for the viewer to handle, a "Too Much Break" is called and written down (objectified), telling the system to slow down and supply information in order of importance. After the overload is dissipated, the viewer may resume from the break, normally with the reiteration of the coordinate. A Too Much Break is often indicated by an overly elaborate ideogram or ideograms.

d.   Aesthetic Impact Break ("AI Break"):   Will be discussed in conjunction with Stage III.

e.   AOL Drive Break (AOL-D Bk):   This type of break becomes necessary when an AOL or related AOLs have overpowered the system and are "driving" the process (as   evidenced by the recurrence of a specific AOL two or more times), producing nothing but spurious information. Once the AOL-Drive is objectified, the break time taken will usually need to be longer than that for a normal AOL to allow the viewer to fully break contact and allow to dissipate the objectionable analytic loop.

f.   Bilocation Break (Bilo Bk):   When the viewer perceives he is too much absorbed in and transferred to the site and cannot therefore appropriately debrief and objectify site information, or that he is too aware of and contained within the here-and-now of the remote viewing room, only weakly connected with the signal line, a Bilo break must be declared and objectified to allow the viewer to back out, and then get properly recoupled with the signal line again.

g.   Break (Break):   If at any point in the system the viewer must take a break that does not fit into any of the other categories, a "Break" is declared.   It has been recommended that a break not be taken if the signal line is coming through strong and clear.   If the break is extensive--say for twenty minutes or more, it is appropriate to objectify "Resume" and the time at the point of resumption.

The viewer declares a break by objectifying "AOL

Break", "AI Break", "Bilo Break", etc., as appropriate, usually in the right hand margin of the paper. Immediately underneath he briefly objectifies in one or a few words the cause or content of what occasioned the necessity for a break.

C. Summary:

Structure is the key to usable RV technology. It is through proper structure-discipline that mental noise is suppressed and signal line information allowed to emerge cleanly. As expressed by one early student, "Structure! Content be damned!" is the universal motto of the remote viewer. As long as proper structure is maintained information obtained may be relied on. If the viewer starts speculating about content--wondering "what it is"--he will begin to depart from proper structure and AOL will inevitably result. One of the primary duties of both monitor and viewer is to insure the viewer maintains proper structure, taking information in the correct sequence, at the correct stage, and in the proper manner.

STAGE I

A. Concept:

Any given site has an overall nature or "gestalt", as it is referred to below, that makes it uniquely what it is. In Stage I, the remote viewer is taught to acquire the signal line, attune himself to it, and proceed to decode and objectify this site gestalt and the major pieces of information that pertain to it. A properly executed Stage I is the very foundation of everything that follows after it, and it is therefore of utmost importance to maintain correct structure and achieve an accurate Stage I concept of the site. All CRV sessions begin with Stage I.

B. Definitions:

1. Major Gestalt: The overall impression presented by all elements of the site taken for their composite interactive meaning. The one concept that more than all others would be the best description of the site.

2. Ideogram: The "I" component of the I/A/B

sequence. The ideogram is the spontaneous graphic representation of the major gestalt, manifested by the motion of the viewer's pen on paper, which motion is produced by the impingement of the signal line on the autonomic nervous system and the reflexive transmission of the resultant nervous energy to the muscles of the viewer's hand and arm. The objectified ideogram has no "scale"; that is, the size of the ideogram relative to the paper seems to have no relevance to the actual size of any component at the site.

3. "A" Component: The "feeling/motion" component of the ideogram. The "feeling/motion" is essentially the impression of the physical consistency (hard, soft, solid, fluid, gaseous, etc.) and contour/shape/motion of the site. For example, the monitor has selected, unknown to the viewer, a mountain as the trainee's site. At the iteration of the coordinate, the trainee produces an appropriate ideogram, and responds verbally, at the same time as he writes it: "Rising up, peak, down." This is the "motion" sensation he experienced as his pen produced the ideogram. He then says "solid" if having experienced the site as being solid as opposed to fluid or airy. This is the "feeling" component of the Stage I process. There are at least five possible types of feelings: solidity, liquidity, energetics, airiness (that is, where there is more air space than anything else, such as some suspension bridges might manifest), and temperature. Other feeling descriptors are possible, but encountered only in rare circumstances and connected with unusual sites. These components and how they are expressed in structure will be discussed more fully below. Though in discussions of theory this aspect is usually

149

addressed as "feeling/motion", it will normally be the case in actual session work that the motion aspects decoded first with the feeling portion coming second.

4. "B" Component: The first (spontaneous) analytic response to the ideogram "A" component.

C. Site Requirements:

For training in Stage I, a stage specific site is selected. Basic Stage I coordinate remote viewing sites generally comprise an area isolated by some five miles on a side and possess easily identifiable major gestalts that may be easily decoded in simple Stage I sessions. All sites have Stage I gestalts, but for training Stage I perceptions these "simple" sites are selected.

D. Types of Ideograms:

There are four types of ideograms:

1. Single: One unbroken mark or line, containing only one "A" component (feeling/motion) and one "B" component.

2. Double: Two basically parallel marks or lines. Produces usually at least three sets of "A" and "B" components: one for the area between the marks, and one each for the areas on either side of the marks. Two other "A" and "B" components may be present as well, one for each of the marks. Railroad tracks, roads, canals, etc. may produce this type of ideogram.

3. Multiple: Two or more different marks, each producing its own set or sets of "A" and "B" components. Such an ideogram may be obtained when there is more than one major gestalt present at a given site--such as a lake, city and mountain--all within the area designated by the coordinate. This type of ideogram may occasion the necessity of taking a "Too Much Break" because of the volume of information contained in more than one major gestalt. Caution must be exercised here, since a single mark may actually represent either a double or a multiple ideogram, but may be mistaken for a single ideogram. To ascertain this, the signal line must be prompted by placing the pen on the mark and also to either side to determine if more than one "A" and "B" component is present.

4. Composite: Pen leaves paper more than twice, makes identical marks, and produces one set of "A" and "B" components. Things such as orchards, antenna fields, etc. with numbers of identical components produce this type of ideogram.

E. Vertical/Horizontal Ideogram Orientation:

Ideograms may be encountered (objectified) either parallel with the plane of the horizon (horizontal) or perpendicular to it (vertical). For example, the Gobi desert being predominantly flat, wavy sand, would produce a motion portion of the Stage I "A" component as "across, flat, wavy", or similar terminology, indicating a horizontal ideogram. The

Empire State Building, however, would produce some sort of vertical response such as "up, angle", in the motion portion of the "A", indicating a vertical ideogram. However, a crucial point to remember is the objectification of the ideogram is completely independent either of what it looks like or its orientation on paper. It is imperative to realize that what determines the vertical/horizontal ideogram orientation is the site's inherent manifestation in the physical world, and not how or what direction it is executed on the paper, or even the RVer's "point of view", since in Stage I there is no viewer site orientation in the dimension lane. Simply observing how the ideogram looks on paper will not give reliable clues as to what the orientation of the ideogram might be. The ideogram objectified as "across, flat, wavy" for the Gobi Desert might on the paper be an up and down mark. The ideogram for the Empire State Building could possibly be represented as oriented across the paper. It is obvious then that ideograms cannot be interpreted by what they "look like", but by the feeling/motion component produced immediately following the ideogram. The viewer must learn to sense the orientation of an ideogram as he executes it. If unsuccessful on the first attempt, the ideogram may be "re-prompted" by moving the pen along it at the same tempo as it was produced, with the viewer being alert to accurately obtain the missing information.

F. I/A/B Formation:

As the monitor gives the prompting information (coordinate, etc.) the viewer writes it down on the left side of the paper, then immediately afterwards places his pen on the paper again to execute the ideogram ("I"). This presents itself as a spontaneous mark produced on the paper by the motion of hand and   pen.

Immediately upon execution of the ideogram, the viewer then moves his pen to the right third of the paper where he writes "A" and describes briefly the feeling/motion characteristics of the site as it is manifest in the ideogram, for example, "Across angle up angle across angle down, solid."

Upon correctly decoding the feeling/motion component, the viewer then moves his pen to a position below the recorded feeling/motion responses and directly under the "A", then writes "B". He then records the appropriate "B" component response, which will be the first instantaneous analytic response following the ideogram and feeling/motion components to the signal line's impingement on his system. Sample responses may be "mountain "water", "structure", "land", "nice", "city", "sand", "swamp", etc.

G. Phases I and II:

Stage I training is divided into two phases, determined by the number and types of major gestalts produced by the site used. Phase I consists of sites evincing only one simple major gestalt, for example, mountain, city, or water. Phase II includes sites with more than one major gestalt, and therefore some sort of identifiable interface: a beach on an ocean, an island, a city by a river, or a mountain with a lake.

H. Drills:

Most viewers tend to establish well worn patterns in executing ideograms on paper. If such habits become established enough, they can actually inhibit proper handling of the signal line by restricting ease and flexibility in proper ideogram production. In order to counter this tendency, training drills may occasionally be conducted. These drills use paper with a large number of rectangles, outlined in black, of different sizes, proportions, and orientations (i.e., with the long sides paralleling in some cases the top of the paper and other cases paralleling the sides of the paper). As he comes to each of these rectangles on the paper in turn, the viewer is directed to execute an ideogram for a given site (i.e., "mountain', "lake", "city", "canyon", "orchard", "island", "mountain by a lake with a city", "waterfall", "volcano", etc.) with his pen inside the rectangle, extending the ideogram as appropriate from one side of the rectangle to another without passing outside the rectangle. Each time the directions may vary--the ideogram will have to be executed from top to bottom, right to left, left to right, bottom to top, diagonally, etc. In the case of ideograms that do not have a directional emphasis, such as one formed by a circle, a grouping of dots, etc., the ideogram must fill the area of the rectangle without going outside it. The ideogram must be executed as rapidly as possible, without any hesitation or time taken to think. The purpose of this exercise is obviously to encourage spontaneity and increase facility with pen on paper; though it is unlikely that real signal line connection occurs, the ideograms created by the near totally reflexive actions involved in the drill approach actual archetypal ideogrammatic styles.

I. Format:

All sessions are begun by writing the viewer's name and the date/time group of the session in the upper right hand corner of the paper, together with any other session relevant information deemed necessary by the monitor. As stated above, the coordinate or other prompting information is written in the left third of the paper. the ideogram approximately in the middle third (though because of the spontaneous nature of the ideogram, it may indeed be executed much closer to the prompting data, sometimes even being connected to it), and the "A" and "B" components in the right third. AOL and other breaks are declared near the right edge of the paper. This format constitutes the structure of Stage I and when properly executed, objectifies (gives reality to) the signal line.

Following is a sample Stage I format: (On next page.)

(FORMAT FOR STAGE I)

Name
Date
Time

(Personal Inclemencies/Advance Visuals Declared)

STAGE I
(Coordinate) (Ideogram)

A: Across, Angle Up, Angle, Angle

Across,

Angle Down, Solid

B: Structure

AOL Break
Sports
stadium

STAGE II

A. Concept:

Stage II presents to the viewer's cognition signal line data relevant to physical sensory input. The classic explanation of this is that such data are exactly equivalent to "sensations the viewer would experience were he physically present at the site." In effect, this allows the viewer to come into closer contact with the signal line through recognition and objectification of sensory facts relevant to the site. This information centers around the five physical senses: touch, smell, sight, sound, and taste, and can include both temperature (both as a tactile "hot/cold to the touch" sensation, and/or a general environmental ambience) and "energetics" (i.e., magnetism, strong radio broadcasts, nuclear radiation, etc.).

B. Definitions:

1. Sense: Any of the faculties, as sight, hearing, smell, taste, or touch, by which man perceives stimuli originating from outside or inside the body.

2. Sensory: Of or pertaining to the senses or sensation.

3. Tactile: Of, pertaining to, endowed with, or affecting the sense of touch. Perceptible to the touch; capable of being touched; tangible.

4. Auditory: Of or pertaining to hearing, to the sense of hearing, or to the organs of hearing. Perceived through or resulting from the sense of hearing.

5. Dimension: Extension in a single line or direction as length, breadth and thickness or depth. A line has one dimension, length. A plane has two dimensions, length and breadth. A solid or cube has three dimensions, length, breadth and thickness.

C. Site Requirements:

Sites for Stage II training are selected for their pronounced manifestation of sensory information. Examples: sewage treatment plant, airport, pulp mill, botanical garden, chocolate factory, steel mill, amusement park, etc.

D. Clusters:

Stage II responses tend to come in groups or "clusters" of words--usually 3-4 words, though sometimes more pertaining to different aspects or gestalts of the site. If for example a body of water and an area of land are present at the site, a group of sensory Stage II words might be produced by the viewer relating to the land, then another group relating to the water. This is particularly noticeable in sites whose ideograms produce two or more "A" and "B" components. Stage IIs will tend to cluster in respect to the "A" and "B" components to which they relate. Stage II responses cluster in another sense as well. Frequently, types of sensory responses will come together. For example two or three tastes, smells, colors, or textures may cluster together as the viewer objectifies his perceptions on the paper.

E. "Basic" Words:

True Stage IIs are generally simple, fundamental words dealing directly with a sensory experience: i.e. rough, red, cold, stinging smell, sandy taste, soft, moist, green, gritty, etc. When objectified words go beyond the "basics" they are considered "out of structure" and therefore unreliable.

F. Aperture:

After a proper Stage I Ideogram/A/B sequence has been executed, the aperture (which was at its narrowest point during Stage I) opens to accommodate Stage II information. Not only does this allow the more detailed sensory information to pass through to the viewer, but it is accompanied by a correspondingly longer signal "loiter" time--the information comes in more slowly, and is less concentrated. Towards the end of Stage II, and approaching the threshold of Stage III, the aperture begins to expand even further, allowing the acquisition of dimensionally related information. (see below).

G. Dimensionals:

As the viewer proceeds through Stage II and approaches Stages III, the aperture widens, allowing the viewer to shift from a global (gestalt) perspective, which is paramount through Stage I and most of Stage II, to a perspective in which certain limited dimensional characteristics are discernible. "Dimensionals" are words produced by the viewer and written down in structure to conceptualize perceived elements of this new dimensional perspective he has now gained through the widening of the aperture. These words demonstrate five dimensional concepts: verticalness, horizontalness, angularity, space or volume, and mass. While at first glance the concept of "mass" seems to be somewhat inappropriate to the dimensional concept, mass in this case can be conceived in dimensionally related terms as in a sense being substance occupying a specific three-dimensional area. Generally received only in the latter portion of Stage II, dimensionals are usually very basic--"tall", "wide", "long", "big". more complex dimensionals such as "panoramic" are usually received at later stages characterized by wider aperture openings.

If these more complex dimensionals, are reported during Stage II they are considered "out of structure" and therefore unreliable.

H. Analytic Overlay (AOL):

Analytic overlay is considerably more rare in Stage II than it is in Stage I. Though it does occasionally occur, something about the extremely basic sensory nature of the data bits being received strongly tends to avoid AOL. Some suppositions suggest that the sensory data received comes across either at a low enough energy level or through a channel that does not stimulate the analytic portion of the mind to action. In effect, the mind is "fooled" into thinking Stage II information is being obtained from normal physical sensory sources. The combination of true sensory data received in Stage II may produce a valid signal line "image" consisting of colors, forms, and textures. Stage II visuals or other true signal line visuals of the site may be distinguished from an AOL in that they are perceived as fuzzy, indistinct and tending to fade in and out as one attempts to focus on its constituent elements rather than the sharp, clear, static image present with AOL.

I. Aesthetic Impact (AI):

Aesthetic impact indicates a sudden and dramatic widening of the aperture, and signals the transition from Stage II into Stage III. In normal session structure, it occurs only after two or more dimensionals occur in the signal line. On occasion, however, AI can occur more or less spontaneously in Stage II, especially when a site is involved with very pronounced Stage II elements, such as a particularly noisome chemical plant. AI is the viewer's personal, emotional response to the site: "How the site makes you feel." It can be a manifestation of sudden surprise, vertigo, revulsion, or pleasure. Though some sites seem to consistently elicit similar AI responses in any person who remote views them, it must still be borne in mind that an AI response is keyed directly to the individuals own personality and emotional/physical makeup, and that therefore AI responses can differ, sometimes dramatically so, from viewer to viewer. AI will be more fully discussed in the section of this paper dealing with Stage III.

J. Drills/Exercises:

To promote flexibility in producing Stage II responses, an exercise is usually assigned viewer trainees. This consists of producing a list of at least sixty sensory response type words, dealing with all the possible categories of sensory perceptions: tastes, sounds, smells, tactile experience, colors and other elementary visuals, and magnetic/energetic experiences. When giving the assignment, the trainer emphasizes reliance on "basic" words as described above.

K. Format:

Following is a sample Stage II format

(FORMAT FOR STAGE II)

Name
Date
Time

(Personal Inclemencies/Advance Visuals Declared)

STAGE I
(Coordinate) (Ideogram)

A: Across, Angle Up, Angle, Angle Across,

Angle Down, Solid

B: Structures

STAGE II **S-2:** White   **AI Break**
(Sensory Data)   Warm   "Smells Gross!"

Unclean smell

**AOL
Break**
"Smells
like dirty air."

STAGE I
(Coordinate) (Ideogram/Multiple)

A: Up, Angle Across, Angle
Down

Solid
B: Structure

A: Angle Across, Angle Down
Solid
B: Structure

A: Flat
Hard
B: Land

STAGE II   **S-2:** Gray
(Sensory Data)   White
      Rough
      Noisy
      Densely populated - S4 *[Note: This is Stage IV data, not II.]*
      Warm Smell of Fumes.

Confusion
Break
"Thud or scraping
sound"
"Can't tell."

STAGE II
(Dimensionals)   **D:** Tall *[Note: This is the start of dimensionals.]*
      High
      Solid
      Wide

AI Break
"Man! This
thing is really BIG!"

STAGE III

A. Concept:

As Stage II progresses the aperture opens dramatically wider than was the case with either Stages I or early Stage II. Dimensionals begin to emerge and the threshold is reached for the transition into Stage III. The shift into full Stage III is triggered by aesthetic impact (see below). It is after this point that the true dimensionality of the site may begin to be expressed. This differs from dimensional elements encountered previously, in that Stage II dimensionals are individual aspects of the site, while Stage III dimensionality is a composite of inherent site aspects. The concept of "the viewer's perspective" must, however, be avoided because in Stage III the viewer has not yet reached the point where complete comprehension and appreciation of the size, shape, and dimensional composition of the overall site can be ascertained. Generally, the viewer himself is not precisely aware of his own perspectual relationship to the site and therefore not consciously aware of the true relationship of all the dimensional components he is able to debrief from Stage III. As is discussed in various sections below, he must rely on the various tools available in Stage III to obtain, and organize the increased information he is perceiving. Although Stage III can provide a great deal of information about any given site, the goal of Stage III is command of structure.

B. Definitions:

1. Aesthetic: Sensitivity of response to given site.

2. Drawing: The act of representing something by line, etc.

3. Idea: Mental conception; a vague impression; a hazy perception; a model or archetype.

4. Impact: A striking together; changes, moods, emotions, sometimes very gross, but may be very weak or very subtle.

5. Mobility: The state or quality of being mobile.

6. Motion: The act or process of moving.

7. Perceptible: That which can be grasped mentally through the senses.

8. Prompt: To incite to move or to action; move or inspire by suggestion.

9. Rendering: Version; translation (often highly detailed).

10. Sketch: To draw the general outline without much detail; to describe the principle points (idea) of.

11. To Track: To trace by means of vestiges, evidence, etc.; to follow with a line.

12. Vision: One of the faculties of the sensorum, connected to the visual senses out of which the brain

constructs an image.

C. Site Requirements:

A site selected for Stage III would logically require significant dimensional components. Locales such as bridges, monuments, airports, unusual natural formations, etc. are useful Stage III sites.

D. The Six Primary Dimensionals:

1. Diagonal: Something that extends between two or more other things; a line connecting two points or intersection of two lines of a figure.

2. Horizontal: Parallel to the plane of the horizon.

3. Mass: Extent of whatever forms a body--usually matter.

4. Space: Distance interval or area between or within things. "Empty distance."

5. Vertical: Perpendicular to the plane of the horizon; highest point/lowest point (i.e., height or depth).

6. Volume: A quantity; bulk; mass; or amount.

E. Aesthetic Impact:

As the aperture widens rapidly from Stage II, a virtual avalanche of site information begins to impact on the viewer's unconscious. The cumulative effect of all this detail is to trigger a subjective response from the viewer. This opening of the aperture and subsequent subjective response is called Aesthetic Impact (AI) and is the viewer's subjective emotional response to the site. It is best described as "how the site makes the viewer feel". AI may immediately follow two Stage II dimensional responses, but it will certainly follow three or more. It may be experienced and expressed in a variety of ways. A simple exclamation of "Wow!" may be the A response when one is suddenly impressed by the immensity of some natural formation, such as the Grand Canyon or Yosemite's Half Dome. On the other hand, such a site might just as easily spark a feeling of vertigo, or fear of falling, or cause one to remark, "This is really tall (or deep)." A pulp mill might trigger an AI reaction of revulsion because of the nauseating smells. Or a comprehension of the grandeur or squalor of a site might cause one to have a sudden appreciation of beauty or ugliness. Other examples of AI might be claustrophobia, loneliness, fright, pleasantness, relaxation, enjoyment, etc.

AI need not be pronounced to be present; in fact, it may often be quite subtle and difficult to recognize. It may sometimes be a sudden, mild cognitive recognition of the abrupt change in perspective, or a slight surprise or alteration of attitude about the site. Some viewers who in the past have had little experience with direct contact with their emotions may have difficulty recognizing that they experience AI, and may even be convinced it doesn't happen to them. Such individuals must exercise a great deal of caution not to sublimate or suppress AI recognition, and require additional exposure to AI to help them learn to recognize and declare it appropriately.

The monitor also has a role to play in helping the viewer to recognize AI. Body language, eye movement, and specific speech patterns can all be cues to the experienced monitor that AI is present. The monitor must draw the viewer's attention to the existence of an undeclared AI when he observes the "symptoms" of an AI unrecognizable to the viewer. It is extremely important to properly recognize and declare (objectify) AI, since how one deals with it can determine the entire course of the session from that point on. The viewer may not work through AI. Aesthetic Impact must be recognized, declared, and allowed to thoroughly dissipate. Should the viewer err and attempt to work through AI, all information from that point on will be colored by the subjective filter of the emotional experience encountered, and AOL Drive and AOL "Peacocking" (discussed under AOL, below) can be expected to arise.

AI is dealt with in the following manner. Moving through Stage II, the viewer begins to debrief a cluster of two or more basic dimensionals. He suddenly realizes that the aperture is expanding, and that in conjunction he is having a subjective emotional reaction to the site--whether pronounced or mild. He then states aloud as he objectifies on his paper "AI Break". He then briefly says aloud and writes on the paper what the AI is. Declarations can be everything from a simple "Wow!" to "Disgusting." to "I like this place" to "Vertigo" to "I feel sick" to "This is boring" to "I'm impressed by how tall this is" to "Absolutely massive!" The viewer by taking this "AI Break" effectively disengages himself temporarily from the signal line and allows the emotional response to dissipate.

The time required for this can vary from a few brief seconds for a mild AI to hours for one that is especially emphatic. It is important to note that, though many sites elicit essentially the same response in every individual who remote views it, each person is different than every other and therefore under certain circumstances and with certain sites AI responses may differ significantly from viewer to viewer. One example of this that has frequently been related is a small sandy spit off of Cape Cod, Massachusetts. One viewer, a highly gregarious woman who enjoys social interactions, when given the site responded that it made her feel bleak, lonesome, depressed, abandoned. On the other hand, a viewer who had spent a great deal of his time in nature and away from large numbers of other humans experienced the site as beautiful and refreshing. Since AI is subjective, such variations are not unexpected, and under the right circumstances usually appropriate.

F. Motion/Mobility:

Two variations of the concept of movement are recognized as being available to the viewer during Stage III. The first is the idea of motion at the site: an object or objects at the site may be observed as they shift position or are displaced from one location to another. For example, there may be automobile traffic present, a train moving through the area, or whirling or reciprocating machinery, etc."Mobility", the second movement concept, is the ability possessed by the viewer in Stage III to shift his viewpoint to some extent from point to point about the site, and from one perspective to another, i.e., further back, closer up, from above, or below, etc.

This ability makes possible the production of trackers and sketches as described below. An additional feature this introduces is the ability to shift focus of awareness from one site to another using a polar coordinate concept. This is more fully explained under Movement/Movement Exercises, which follows.

G. Dimensional Expression on Paper:

1. Sketches:

a. Spontaneous sketches: With the expansion of the aperture and after dissipation of AI, the viewer is prepared to make representations of the site dimensional aspects with pen on paper. A sketch is a rapidly executed general idea of the site. In some cases it may be highly representational of the actual physical appearance of the site, yet in other cases only portions of the site appear. The observed accuracy or aesthetic qualities of a sketch are not particularly important. The main function of the sketch is to stimulate further intimate contact with the signal line while continuing to aid in the suppression of the viewer's subjective analytic mental functionings. Sketches are distinguished from drawings by the convention that drawings are more deliberate, detailed representations and are therefore subject to far greater analytic (and therefore AOL producing) interpretation in their execution.

b. Analytic sketches: Analytic sketches are produced using a very carefully controlled analytic process usually employed only when a satisfactory spontaneous sketch as described above is not successfully obtained. An analytic sketch is obtained by first listing all dimensional responses obtained in the session, including those contained in the "A" components of the various coordinate I/A/B prompting sequences, in the order and frequency they manifest themselves on the session transcript. Each of these dimensional elements apparently manifests itself in order of its importance to the gestalt of which it is a part. So, for example, if in the first "A" component of the session one encounters "across, rising", these two would head the list, and their approximate placement on the paper will be determined by the viewer before any other. A second list is then compiled, listing all secondary attributes of the site. Finally, a list may be made if desired of any significant "details" that do not fit into the previous two categories.

In analytic sketching the intuitive part of the viewer's apparatus is not shut off. He must continue to attempt to "feel" the proper placement of the dimensional elements of the site. In fact, the purpose of this approach to sketching is to "reignite" the viewer's intuition. As each element on the primary list is taken in order, the viewer must "feel" the proper position for that element in relation to the others. If the dimensional element "round" is listed, it must be determined how a rounded element fits in with "across", "rising", "flat", "wide", "long", and any other dimensional elements that may have preceded it. When elements from the primary list are exhausted, the viewer may duplicate the process with those from the secondary list. If necessary and desirable, the viewer may proceed to the details list and assign them their appropriate locations.

2. Trackers:

Stage III contact with the site may on occasion produce an effect known as a tracker. This is executed by a series of closely spaced dots or dashed lines made by pen on paper and describes a contour, profile, or other dimensional aspect of the site. Trackers are formed in a relatively slow and methodical manner. The viewer holds pen in hand, lifting it off the paper between each mark made, thereby allowing the autonomic nervous system, through which the signal line is being channeled, to determine the placement of each successive mark. While constructing a tracker, it is possible for the viewer to spontaneously change from executing the tracker to executing a sketch, and back again.

3. Spontaneous Ideograms:

At any point in the sketch/tracker process ideogram may spontaneously occur. This most probably relates to a sub-gestalt of the site, and should be treated like any other ideogram. It will produce "A" and "B" components, S-2s, and so forth. Because of the possibility for the occurrence of these spontaneous ideograms with their potential for conveying additional important site information, viewers are strongly counseled to always keep their pen on paper to the greatest extent practical.

H. Movement/Movement Exercises:

An outgrowth of the viewer mobility concept involves the ability of the viewer to shift his focus from one site to other sites using a polar coordinate concept.

This is often termed "S-2 movement" or "movement exercise", and is executed thusly. The viewer is given the coordinates for the base site, and the session proceeds as normal: I/A/B, S-2s, dimensionals, AI to Stage III sketches/trackers. When the monitor is confident that the viewer has successfully locked onto this primary site, he tells the viewer to "prepare for movement." The viewer accordingly places his pen on the left side of the paper, indicating he is ready for a new prompting coordinate as per convention. The monitor then tells the viewer to acquire the central site. The viewer responds with a very brief, few word description of the base site, whereupon the monitor gives a prompting statement in lieu of the usual geographic coordinate. This statement includes a distance and direction from the base site, and is couched in words as neutral, passive and non-suggestive (therefore less AOL inducing) as possible.

By way of example, let us assume that the base site is a large gray structure, and the secondary site to which the viewer's focus is to be moved is 8 1/2 miles northwest of the base site. The monitor will say "Acquire the site", to which the viewer responds approximately, "a large gray structure." The monitor then says 8 1/2 miles (to the) northwest something should be visible. Just as he would a geographic coordinate, the viewer objectifies this phrase by writing it down, places his pen on the paper to receive the ideogram, and progresses from there just as if he were processing any other new site.

Note, however, the very neutral way the monitor provided the prompting. He avoided such leading words as, "What do you see 8 1/2 miles northwest?"

174

or "You should be able to see (hear/feel/smell) something 8 1/2 miles northwest." observe also that "motion words" ("move", "shift", "go", etc.) were also avoided. Words and phraseology of either type tends to cause the viewer to take an active role, directly attempting to perceive the site instead of letting the signal line bring the information to him. This sort of active involvement greatly encourages the development of AOL and other mental noise effects. Instead, the passive wording used by the monitor stimulates by the analytic component of the mind as little as possible, allowing uncontaminated signal line data to be received. Examples of acceptable passively framed words relating to sensory involvement are, "should be visible", "hearable", "smellable", "feelable", "tasteable", etc. In earlier stages sensory based wording would have been avoided as a catalyst to AOL. With the widened aperture in Stage III, however it may be used successfully.

This movement technique may be used any number of times, starting either from the original base site, or from one of the other subsequent sites to which the viewer's perception has been "moved".

I. Analytic Overlay (AOL) in Stage III:

1. AOL Matching:

With the expansion in aperture inherent in Stage III, and after appropriate AI, the AOL phenomenon develops to where a viewer's AOL may match or nearly match the actual signal line impression of the site. For example, if the site were Westminster Abbey, the viewer might produce the AOL of Notre

Dame cathedral. Or he might even actually get an image of Westminster Abbey that nevertheless fills all the criteria for an AOL.

According to theory, the matching AOL is superimposed over the true signal line. It is however possible with practice to distinguish the vague parameters of the true signal line "behind" the bright, distinct, but somewhat translucent image of the AOL. The viewer must become proficient at "seeing through" the AOL to the signal line. Use of "seeing through" here must not be taken to imply any visual image in the accepted sense of the word, but rather as a metaphor best describing the perceptory effect that manifests itself.

2. AOL Drive:

Although mentioned before, AOL Drive becomes a serious concern beginning in Stage III. It occurs when the viewer's system is caught up in an AOL to the extent that the viewer at least temporarily believes he is on the signal line, even though he is not. When two or more similar AOLs are observed in close proximity, AOL drive should be suspected. AOL drive is indicated by one or more of the following: repeating signals; signal line ending in blackness; peculiar (for that particular viewer) participation in the signal line; and/or peacocking. Causes for AOL drive include accepting a false "B" component in Stage I; or accepting a false sketch or undeclared AOL in Stage III. Undeclared AOLs can spawn AOL drive in all other stages beyond Stage III as well. Once it is realized that AOL drive is present, the viewer should take an "AOL Break" (as discussed under STRUCTURE) , then review his data to determine at what point he accepted the AOL as legitimate data. After a sufficient break the viewer should resume the session with the data obtained before the AOL drive began. Listed below are two subspecies of AOL drive.

a. Ratcheting: The recurrence of the same AOL over and over again as if trapped in a feedback loop.

b. AOL "Peacocking:" The rapid unfolding, one right after another, of a series of brilliant AOLs, each building from the one before, analogous to the unfolding of a peacock's tail.

J. Format:

Following is a sample format for Stage III:

(FORMAT FOR STAGE III)

Name
Date
Time

(Personal Inclemencies/Visuals Declared)

STAGE I
(Coordinate) (Ideogram)

> **A:** Rising
> Angle
> Across
> Down
> Solid
> **B:** Structures

STAGE II　　　**S-2:** Gray

(Sensory Data)
                              White
                              Rough
                              Gritty Texture
                              Noisy Mixture of Sounds
                              Warm
                              Moist
                              Smell of Fumes
                              Unclean Smell
                              Hazy

STAGE II
(Dimensionals)   **D:** Tall *(beginning of dimensionals leading to AI and Stage III sketching/ tracking)*

                              Wide
                              Long
                              Huge

                                        AI
                                        BREAK
                                        "Wow!
                                        I'm dizzy!"

STAGE III
(Sketch or Tracker)

                                        AOL
                                        BREAK
                                        Empire
                                        State Building

STAGE IV

A. Concept:

With the successful accomplishment of Stage I-II, the viewer has become subject to an enormous flood of information available from the site. Previously, such a flow of data would have been overwhelming, and those circumstances in Stages I through III in which the viewer found himself so inundated would have required the taking of a "Too Much Break." At this point, however, it becomes both possible and necessary to (1) establish a systematic structure to provide for the orderly, consistent management of the volumes of information that may be obtained, and (2) facilitate and guide the viewer's focusing of perceptions on ever finer and finer detail of the site. This is accomplished through the use of an information matrix which is illustrated below. Stage IV is a refinement and expansion of the previous structure to facilitate more complete and detailed

179

decoding of the signal line.

B. Definitions:

Most of the terms used in a Stage IV matrix have been defined previously. Those that have not are explained as follows:

1. Emotional Impact: The perceived emotions or feelings of the people at the site or of the viewer. Sometimes the site itself possesses an element of emotional impact, which is imprinted with long or powerful associations with human emotional response.

2. Tangibles: Objects or characteristics at the site which have solid, "touchable" impact on the perceptions of the viewer, i.e., tables, chairs, tanks, liquids, trees, buildings, intense smells, noises, colors, temperatures, machinery, etc.

3. Intangibles: Qualities of the site that are perhaps abstract or not specifically defined by tangible aspects of the site, such as purposes, non-physical qualities, categorizations, etc.; i.e., "governmental", "foreign", "medical", "church", administrative", "business", "data processing", "museum", "library", etc.

4. AOL/S: Virtually synonymous with the previously considered term "AOL Matching", AOL/Signal occurs when an AOL produced by the viewer's analytic mental machinery almost exactly matches the site, and the viewer can to some extent "look" through the AOL image to perceive the actual site. The advantage of AOL/S in Stage IV is that it allows the information to be used without calling a break. One can ask, "What is this trying to tell me about the site?" As an example, the viewer may perceive the Verazzano Narrows Bridge when in fact the site is actually the George Washington Bridge.

5. Dimensionals: "Dimensionals" have an even broader meaning here than in Stage III. In Stage IV, more detailed and complex dimensionals can be expected and are now considered to be in structure and therefore more reliable. "Spired", "twisted", "edged", "partitioned", etc. are only a few examples.

C. Stage IV Matrix:

To provide the necessary structure for coherent management of this information, matrix column headings are constructed across the top of the paper thusly:

S-2   D   AI   EI   T   I   AOL   AOL/S

These headings stand for the following:

1. **S-2:** Stage II information (sensory data).

2. **D:** Dimensionals.

3. **AI:** Aesthetic Impact.

4. **EI:** Emotional Impact.

5. **T:** Tangibles.

6. **I:** Intangibles.

7. **AOL:** Analytic Overlay.

8. **AOL/S:** AOL/Signal.

D. Session Format and Mechanics:

As the viewer produces Stage IV responses (generally single words that describe the concepts received via the signal line) are entered in the matrix under their appropriate categories. The matrix is filled in left to right, going from the more sense base Stage IIs and dimensional towards the ever more refined information to the right, and top to bottom, following the natural flow of the signal line. Stage IV information, similar to that of Stage II, comes to the viewer in clusters. Some particular aspect of the signal will manifest itself, and the sub-elements pertaining to that aspect, will occur relatively rapidly to the viewer in the general right-to-left and top-to-bottom pattern just described. Some degree of vertical spacing can be expected between such clusters, an indication that each of these clusters represents a specific portion of the site.

Entries in a properly filled-in matrix will tend to move slantwise down the page from the upper left to lower right with some amount of moving back and forth from column to column. Stage IIs and dimensionals retain their importance in site definition, while AOLs and AIs, once they have been recognized and objectified, as such, do not require a major interruption in the flow of the signal line as was the case in previous stages. In fact, AOLs now frequently become closely associated with the site and may lead directly to "AOL matching", or

AOL/Signal, as it is categorized in the matrix and described above. EI tends to manifest itself comparatively more slowly than information in other categories. if people are present, for example, EI pertaining to them may be effectively retrieved by placing the pen in the EI column of the matrix. Several moments of subsequent waiting may then be required for the signal to build and deliver its available information. Tangibles will frequently produce immediate sketches or ideograms, which lead to yet more intimate contact with the signal line.

Some degree of control over the order of information retrieval from the signal line can be exercised by the viewer, determined by which column he chooses to set his pen to paper. This acts as a prompting mechanism to induce the signal line to provide information pertinent to the column selected. For example, if more intangibles relating to the site are desired, the pen may be placed in the "I" column to induce the extraction of intangible information from the signal line.

The Stage IV process can be very rapid, and care must be taken to accurately decode and record the data as it comes. However, if as sometimes happens the signal flow should slow, it is recommended that resting the pen on paper in the "EI" column may enhance retrieval of "EI" information, which in turn may potentially stimulate further signal line activity and acquisition.

E. Format:

A sample format for Stage IV follows: (On the next page.)

(FORMAT FOR STAGE IV)

Name
Date
Time

(Personal Inclemencies/Visuals Declared)

STAGE I

(Coordinate) (Ideogram) **A:** Rising
Angle Across
Down, Solid
B: Structures

STAGE II

(Sensory Data)

S2: Rough
Smooth
Gritty Texture
Gray
White
Red
Blue
Yellow
Orange
Clean Taste
Mixture of Smells
Warm
Bright
Noisy

STAGE II

(Dimensionals)

D: Tall

AI BREAK

'interesting' 'I like it here'

"Interesting."
"I like it here."

STAGE III

184

(Sketch or Tracker)

STAGE IV

S-2   D   AI   EI   T   I   AOL
AOL/S

                                        Structures

Rough
Smooth

                                            Manmade

         High
         Tall

                        AI Break:
                        This place is neat!
                                    Doors
                                    Windows
                                        Colorful
                                        Parapets
(Sketch)

                                            Foreign Feeling
                                            People
                            Somber
                            Serious
                            Devoted
                            Enthusiastic
                                    Secular
                                            AOL
                                    BREAK
                                            A castle in
                            a city
                        church.

                                    Notre Dame
                                    Cathedral

STAGE V

A. Concept:

Stage V is unique among the remote viewing stages thus far discussed in that it does not rely on a direct link to the signal line to obtain the information reported. Instead, data is derived through accessing the information already available below the liminal threshold in the brain and autonomic nervous system.

This information is deposited in earlier stages when the signal line passes through the system and "imprints" data on the brain by causing cognitrons to form through the rearrangement of the brain's neuronal clusters into the appropriate patterns, roughly analogous to what occurs in a computer's memory storage when it receives a data dump.

Information "stored" in a cognitron can be accessed

by a certain prompting methodology. In normal brain functioning, cognitrons are induced to deliver up the information they store through some stimulus delivered by the brain, much in the same way as a capacitor in an electronic circuit can be triggered to release its stored electric charge.

When properly prompted, the information released consists of sub-elements which together form the complete cognitron. For example, the concept "religious" may be represented by one complete cognitron (cluster of neurons); each neuron would store a sub-element of that cognitron. Hence, the cognitron for "religious" could have neurons storing data for the following elements: "quiet", "incense", "harmonious chanting", "bowed heads", "robes", "candles", "dimly lit", "reverence", "worship", "respect", etc. If attention is paid to what underlies the concept of "religious" as it is originally evoked in Stage IV, the sub-elements, which may themselves provide valuable information far beyond their collective meaning of "religious", may be broken out and assembled. These sub-elements as they are brought forth in Stage V are known as "emanations" ("emanate" literally defined means "to issue from a source, to flow forth, to emit, or to issue").

B. Definitions:

1. Objects: An object is a thing that can be seen or touched. "Objects" can be understood as those physical items present at the site that helped cause the cognitron to form in the viewer's mind and hence prompt his response of "religious", i.e., "robes", "candles", "incense", etc.

2. Attributes: An attribute is a characteristic or quality of a person or thing. "Attributes" applies to those characteristics of the site that contributed to cognitron formation and the aforementioned viewer response: "quiet", "dimly lit", "echoing", "large", etc.

3. Subjects: "Subject" is defined as something dealt with in a discussion, study, etc. "Subjects" are emanations that might serve a nominative function in describing the site, or be abstract intangibles, or they could be more specific terms dealing with function, purpose, nature, activities, inhabitants, etc., of the site: in the above example, "reverence", "worship", "respect", "harmonious chanting", etc.

4. Topics: "Topic" is defined as a subject of discourse or of a treatise; a theme for discussion. Closely related to "subjects", "topics" often prove to be sub-elements of one or more of the subjects already listed, and frequently are quite specific: "mass", "Catholic", "priest", "communion" , and so forth. An interesting phenomenon to be here considered is that just as one of the subjects encountered may produce several topics, a topic itself may in turn be considered as a subject and produce topics of its own. This construction appears to be very hierarchical and "fractalized", with larger cognitrons being subdivided into smaller ones, which in turn can be further divided, and so on. In fact, any emanation thus "broken out", or "stage-fived" can itself often be further "stage-fived", and subdivided into its own object/attribute/subject/topic categories.

C. Format and Structure:

188

Because extreme caution must be exercised to avoid phrases or promptings that might either induce AOL or otherwise unnecessarily engage the viewer's analytic mental processes, a sort of "hypo-stimulative" type of referral system must be used to "target" the viewer. This is accomplished by dividing the possible types of emanations obtainable into four categories: objects, attributes, subjects, and topics, then prompting the release of subliminally held information by saying and writing "Emanations", followed only by a question mark.

In actual execution, the Stage V format would look somewhat as follows:

Religious Objects
Emanations?

Robes
Candles
Incense

        Religious Attributes
        Emanations?

        Quiet
        Dimly Lit
        Echoing
        Large

                Religious Subjects
                Emanations?

                Worship
                Reverence

Religious
Topics
Emanations
?

Mass
Catholic
Priest
Communion

Note the arrangement of the prompters. First is written the word or concept being broken out. Directly under it is the particular category to be considered.

Finally comes the word "emanations", followed by a question mark. This methodology was developed as the best means of directing a query into the neural "data storage area" of the subconscious without inadvertent hinting", suggestion, or engagement of analytic processes. The word "emanations" represents the sub-elements or component parts of the "religious" cognitron which emerged from the subconscious as a collective concept for these sub-elements. Because it possesses the combined neural energy of the aforementioned components, during Stage IV the overall cognitron-concept is able to pass into the conscious awareness of the viewer with relative ease. The sub-elements themselves, however, have insufficient impetus to individually break unaided through the liminal barrier into the consciousness of the viewer, and must intentionally be invoked through the Stage V process.

It is suspected that the most amount of information will probably be derived from attribute or topic categories, though at times both object and subject headings might provide significant volumes of information. If, as occasionally may happen, all four categories are prompted and no responses result, it can be supposed that one of two situations exist: the response being Stage is either already at its lowest form, or it is really AOL.

D. Implications:

The value of Stage V is readily apparent. Though the sum total of the information obtained quite validly might produce the overall cognitron of "religious" in the context of an RV session, once rendered down to its sub-elements and details the cognitron produces a wealth of additional information of use to the analyst.

E. Considerations:

The process has a few peculiarities and a few cautions to observe. First, one must be aware that not every cognitron necessarily produces responses for every category, and in those that do, some categories are inevitably more heavily represented than others. In general, the rule is that if the list of words that the viewer produces under the particular category being processed does not flow smoothly, regularly, rapidly, and with obvious spontaneity, the end of accessible

information has been reached. Therefore, if there is a pause after the last word recorded of more than a few seconds, the end of the cluster has probably been reached. On the other hand, if after the original prompting nothing comes forth spontaneously, there are probably no accessible emanations pertaining to the cognitron being processed in that category. For example, if the viewer just sits with pen on paper, with nothing to objectify after the viewer has written "religious", "topics" (or other category) and "emanations?" then topic-type information was probably not relevant to the formation of that cognitron. If such a situation should occur either at the beginning of a category or at the end of one more productive, the viewer should either on his own or with encouragement from the monitor declare an end to that particular category and move on the next. Usually, the viewer is intuitively aware when more valid information remains to be retrieved and when the end of a cluster has been reached. To sit too long waiting for more information if none is readily available engages the analytic process and encourages the generation of AOL..

The viewer must also be aware that some responses might at one time or another appear in any one or more of the category columns. One example frequently given is "warm." Although one might consider this an attribute of some object-related word, as a concept of temperature "warm" could just as well show up in the "object" column itself; "electronic", on the other hand, is unlikely to be an object, but could easily fit into attribute, subject or topic columns.

F. Switches:

The "switch" is another issue that needs to be

properly understood in conjunction with the Stage V process. Sometimes, the viewer will be busily recording a string of emanations under a particular category when suddenly emanations from another category intrude.

For example:

Religious Objects
Emanations?

Robes
Candles
Hall
Quiet
Long
Dimly lit
Echoing...

Notice that a few "object" words come through at first, to be replaced spontaneously by words more appropriate to the attribute category. This is known as a "switch"--a point in a Stage V chain where a sudden switch is made from one category to another. There are several possible causes for this. The first is that the viewer has in a sense skipped down a level in detail, and proceeds to provide sub-elements of information for the last valid item in the category--in the above example the words quiet, long, etc., are attributes of "hall", instead of objects belonging to religious."

A second possibility is that all emanations of a given category are exhausted without the viewer being conscious of the fact, and emanations from another category begin to intrude out of proper structure, as shown below:

Robes
Candles
Soothing
Dim
Peaceful
Decorated

Finally, it may be the case that no emanations of the proper type might manifest themselves, but only intruders from another category. Such a situation would indicate that no emanations, of the sort that would be expected for the prompted category are present, and that such emanations were obviously not important in the formation of the cognitron being "stage-fived".

To deal with a switch, one must task the system (after analyzing what has happened) using an alternative category suggested by the trend in the data line. In other words, if attributes are produced by the switch, one should shift to the attributed category and re-prompt the word/cognitron under examination.

G. AOL and Stage V:

Objects and Attributes may be considered "objective elements", in that like Stage IIs, these responses are much less likely to spark AOLS. Topics and Subjects, on the other hand, are "subjective, informational elements", and require special attention to avoid AOL contamination.

AOL, too, may lend itself to being "stage-fived". It

is axiomatic in this RV theory system that analytic overlay is generally valid, site-related information which the analytic centers of the brain have simply taken and "embroidered" with memory associations and suggestive imagery. This implies that accurate information can possibly be derived from an AOL through the Stage V process. For the purposes of Stage V, these kernels of valid site-information are called "prior emanations." The format for "stage-fiving" AOLs is as follows:

AOL mosque
Prior Emanations?

Large
Assembly
Religious decoration
Singing
Reverence
Scriptures
Clergy

When prompting valid prior emanations from an AOL, it is important to indicate only "AOL", and not say or write "AOL Break" as the viewer has been conditioned to do in most other circumstances involving AOL, since the word "break" is intended both to disengage the viewer from the signal line and to inform the viewer's system that the material occasioning the "break" was not desirable.

The prior emanations that result from "stage-fiving" an AOL tend to be a mixture of the four Stage V categories, selected words of which could presumably further be "stage-fived."

Finally, when normal AOL is encountered in the course of a Stage V cluster, which it sometimes is, it should be declared according to normal practice, and the category re-prompted if deemed appropriate, such AOL could no doubt also be subjected to Stage V reduction.

H. Format:

A sample format for Stage V follows: (On the next page.)

(FORMAT FOR STAGE V)

Name
Date
Time

(Personal Inclemencies/Visuals Declared)

STAGE I

(Coordinate) (Ideogram) **A:** Rising
Angle Across
Down, Solid
B: Structures

STAGE II

(Sensory Data) **S-2:** Rough
Smooth
Gritty Texture
Gray
White
Red
Blue
Yellow
Orange
Clean Taste
Mixture of Smells
Warm
Bright
Noisy

STAGE II

(Dimensionals) **D:** Tall
Rounded
Wide
Long
Open

197

AI
BREAK

"Interesting."
"I like
it here."

STAGE III
(Sketch or Tracker)

STAGE IV

S-2	D	AI	EI	T	I	AOL
AOL/S						

Structures

Rough
Smooth
Manmade
   High
   Tall
   Wide
     AI BREAK:
     This place is neat.
        Doors
        Windows
          Colorful
       Parapets
       Building

(Sketch)

Foreign Feeling

People
Somber

Serious
Devoted
Enthusiastic

S-2	D	AI	EI	T	I	AOL
AOL/S						

Secular

AOL Break :
A castle in a city.

A church.

STAGE V

Religious Objects
Emanations?
Robes
Candles
Incense

       Religious Attributes
       Emanations?
       Quiet
       Dimly Lit
       Echoing
       Large

              Religious Subjects
              Emanations?
              Worship
              Reverence
              Respect
              Harmonious

Chanting

Religious Topics
Emanations?
Mass
Catholic
Priest
Communion

AOL
Mosque
Prior
Emanations
?
Large
Assembly
Religious
Decorations
Singing
Reverence
Scriptures
Clergy

STAGE VI

A. Concept:

Stage VI involves the three-dimensional modeling of the site. As such, it is in a sense the continuation of expression of the site's physical characteristics begun in Stage III. Stage VI modeling is a kinesthetic activity which appears to both quench the desire to produce AOL and act as a prompt to produce further information relating to the site--including not just the physical aspects being modeled, but other elements not directly associated with the modeling itself.

B. Functions of Modeling:

Stage VI modeling, has two functions:

1. Kinesthetic interaction with the site by describing

the site with 3-dimensional materials, which facilitates the assessment of relative temporal* and spatial dimensional elements of the site, and;

*NOTE: *An example of relative temporal assessment would be describing a site as being contemporary and modern, with an old world ambience, which the people of today visit to understand the past.*

2. Kinesthetic interaction with the site which effectively lowers the liminal threshold of the viewer by narrowing the RVer's attention field to specific locales (time/space). (Kinesthetic activity is space/time activity, such as moving an object from point A to point B. Not only has the object moved in space, it has also taken time to make the move. Everything in the physical universe is because of kinesthetic activity.)

C. RV Modality:

There are two types of kinesthetic activities in remote viewing--the detect mode and the decode mode. The detect mode includes those behaviors that act as progressively engineered stimuli to the RVer, which in Stage I involves writing the coordinate and in Stage III involves the rendering of a sketch, drawing, or tracker. In Stage VI this mode is represented by 3-dimensional model constructing. Decode kinesthetics, on the other hand, are objectifications which act as responses to the stimuli of the detect mode. Representing the decode mode are the Stage I ideogram, Stage II basics, Stage III dimensionals, the Stage IV matrix, and the Stage VI matrix, all of which are produced from the signal line. Stage V is neither detect nor decode as Stage V information comes from cognitrons formed subconsciously rather than from the signal line.

D. Discussion:

According to theory, as the viewer proceeds through the earlier Stages, his contact with the site is enhanced in quality and increased in extent. Stage VI involves the viewer in direct 3-dimensional modeling and assessment of the site and/or the relationship of Site "T" elements, one to another.

Stage VI may be engaged at several different junctures: after completion of Stage IV and/or Stage V. It can also be entered when Stage IV has stabilized, appropriate AI has been encountered and dealt with, and the viewer has become localized on a specific aspect of the site. Because Stage IV data is collected by "winking" around the site, thereby providing incongruent information, the stabilization/localization must occur prior to Stage VI. After the Stage IV "T" has been modeled, the session can proceed moving to Stage V or by continuing further with Stage VI.

E. Session Mechanics:

As soon as the decision is made to proceed into Stage VI the viewer places in front of him the modeling material (usually clay) that has been kept nearby since the start of the session. At the same time, he also takes a blank piece of paper and writes a Stage VI Matrix on it. As the viewer proceeds to manipulate the modeling material into the form(s), dimensions, and relationships that "feel" right to him, he maintains as his concentrated effort the perception of the site details that are freed to emerge into his consciousness by the kinesthetic experience of the modeling process. These site data are recorded in their appropriate columns on the matrix as the Stage VI portion of the session continues.

1. Matrix: The Stage VI Matrix is identical in form to the Stage IV Matrix:

S-2 D   AI   EI   T   I   AOL   AOL/S

However, it is labeled "Stage VI" for both record keeping purposes and because that matrix pertains to a specific locale in time/space and not the entire site.

2. Considerations: In practice, the viewer constructs the Stage VI Matrix, sets it aside, constructs a 3-dimensional model of Stage IV "T's", and records information perceived from the signal line. During the modeling process, the viewer must:

> a. Focus his awareness on the signal line (not the model) and the information which will begin to slow as the model is constructed, and;

> b. Objectify that information within the prepared Stage VI Matrix. The viewer must keep in mind that the model does not have to be a precise or accurate rendering. It is the objectified information resulting from the modeling that is IMPORTANT.

F. Format:

Following is the format for a typical Stage VI session: (On the next page.)

(FORMAT FOR STAGE VI)

STAGE VI
(This matrix is filled in while viewer is constructing the model.)

S-2	D	AI	EI	T	I	AOL
AOL/S						

				Church		
				Hand-hewn		
				stones		
Gray						
Rough						
very large						

Very Old
War Damaged
Monument
Dreary Climate
International Feeling
Rubble
Separate Structure

Tall
Straight
Rectangular
High
Wide

AI BREAK
"This is really neat!"
"It feels very familiar."
"Modern."
"Same purpose as other structure."
"Church."

"New church and old church are the same."

VIEWER'S SUMMARY:

Site is composed of two churches. One church, which is old and made of hand-hewn stones, has been damaged by war. There is a lot of rubble around it. The new church is very modern in design. Both are located in an area with a cosmopolitan atmosphere and an international flavor. The older church has been left as a monument to remind the people of today of the war atrocities of the past. The new church now serves the same purpose as the older church did at one time--a house of worship.

*NOTE: At the end of a session, the viewer will often produce a short summary of the data contained in session structure as an aid in tying together the information derived from the signal line.

FEEDBACK NOTE: Site is the new Kaiser Wilhelm Church and the war-torn older Kaiser Wilhelm Church, which are side-by-side in Berlin, Germany. The older church, demolished by bombing during World War II, has been left to stand as a monument and a reminder to all who visit.

GLOSSARY

Absorption: Assimilation, as by incorporation or by the digestive process.

"A" Component: The "feeling/motion" component of the ideogram. The "feeling/motion" is essentially the impression of the physical consistency (hard, soft, solid, fluid, gaseous, etc.) and contour/shape/motion of the site.

Aesthetic: Sensitivity of response to given site.

Analytic Overlay (AOL): Subjective interpretation of signal line data, which may or may not be relevant to the site; the analytic response of the viewer's mind to signal line input. An AOL is usually wrong, especially in early stages, but often does possess valid elements of the site that are contained in the signal line.

AOL Drive: This occurs when the viewer's system is caught up in an AOL to the extent that the viewer at least temporarily believes he is on the signal line, even

though he is not. When two or more similar AOLs are observed in close proximity, AOL drive should be suspected. AOL drive is indicated by one or more of the following: repeating signals; signal line ending in blackness; peculiar (for that particular viewer) participation in the signal line; and/or peacocking.

AOL Matching: The viewer must become proficient at "seeing through" the AOL to the signal line. Use of "seeing through" here must not be taken to imply any visual image in the accepted sense of the word, but rather as a metaphor best describing the perceptory effect that manifests itself.

AOL Signal (AOL/S): (Stage IV) Virtually synonymous with "AOL Matching," AOL/Signal occurs when an AOL produced by the viewer's analytic mental machinery almost exactly matches the site, and the viewer can to some extent "look" through the AOL image to perceive the actual site.

Aperture: An opening or open space; hole, gap, cleft, chasm, slit. In radar, the electronic gate that controls the width and dispersion pattern of the radiating signal or wave.

Attributes: An attribute is a characteristic or quality of a person or thing. "Attributes" applies to those characteristics of the site that contributed to cognitron formation and viewer response: "quiet", "dimly lit", "echoing", "large", etc.

Auditory: Of or pertaining to hearing, to the sense of hearing, or to the organs of hearing. Perceived through or resulting from the sense of hearing.

Automatic vs. Autonomic: Reception and movement of the signal line information through the viewer's system and into objectification is an autonomic process as opposed to an automatic one, which itself implies an action arising and subsiding entirely within the system rather than from without.

Autonomic Nervous System (ANS): A part of the vertebrate nervous system that innervates smooth and cardiac muscle and glandular tissues, governs actions that are more or less automatic, and consists of the sympathetic nervous system and the parasympathetic nervous system.

"B" Component: The first (spontaneous) analytic response to the ideogram and "A" component.

Break: The mechanism developed to allow the system to be put on "hold," providing the opportunity to flush out AOLs, deal with temporary inclemencies, or make system adjustments, allowing a fresh start with new momentum. There are seven types of breaks: analytic overlay (AOL), aesthetic impact (AI), AOL-Drive (AOLD), personal inclemency (PI), bilocation (Bilo), confusion (Conf), and too much (TM).

Coding/Encoding/Decoding: The information conveyed on the signal line is "encoded," that is translated into an informational system (a code) allowing data to be "transmitted" by the signal line. Upon receiving the signal, the viewer must "decode" this information through proper structure to make it accessible. This concept is very similar to radio propagation theory, in which the main carrier signal is modulated to convey the desired information.

Cognitron: A cognitron is an assemblage of neurons, linked together by interconnecting synapses, and which when stimulated by the mind's recall system produce a

composite concept of their various subparts. Each neuron is charged with an element of the overall concept, which when combined with the elements of its fellow neurons produces the final concept which the cognitron represents. As a human learns new facts, skills or behaviors, neurons are connecting into new cognitrons, the connecting synapses of which are more and more reinforced with use.

Conscious: Perceiving, apprehending, or noticing with a degree of controlled thought or observation; recognizing as existent, factual, or true. Recognizing as factual or existent something external. Present especially to the senses. Involving rational power, perception, and awareness.

Coordinate: Any one of a set of numbers used in specifying the location of a point on a line, in space, or on a given plane or other surface (latitude and longitude).

Coordinate Remote Viewing (CRV): The process of remote viewing using geographic coordinates for cueing or prompting. (See remote viewing entry below.)

Diagonal: Something that extends between two or more other things; a line connecting two points of intersection of two lines of a figure.

Dimension: Extension in a single line or direction as length, breadth and thickness or depth. A line has one dimension, length. A plane has two dimensions, length and breadth. A solid or cube has three dimensions, length, breadth and thickness.

Drawing: The act of representing something by line, etc.

Emanations: The neuronal inputs that helped form cognitrons producing conscious responses in remote viewing. Emanations can be evoked, decoded, and objectified in the Stage V process.

Emotional Impact: (Stage IV) The perceived emotions or feelings of the people at the site or of the viewer. Sometimes the site itself possesses an element of emotional impact, which is imprinted with long or powerful associations with human emotional response.

Evoking: (evoke: "to call forth or up; to summon; to call forth a response; elicit".) Iteration of the coordinate or alternate prompting method is the mechanism which "evokes" the signal line, calling it up, causing it to impinge on the autonomic nervous system and unconsciousness for transmittal through the viewer and on to objectification.

Feedback: Those responses provided to the viewer during sessions in the early stages of the remote viewing training process to indicate if he has detected and properly decoded site-relevant information; or, information provided at some point after completion of the RV session or project to "close the loop" as it were, providing the viewer with closure as to the site accessed and allowing him to assess the quality of his performance more accurately.

First-Time Effect: In any human activity or skill a phenomenon exists known as "beginner's luck." In coordinate remote viewing, this phenomenon is manifest as especially successful performance at the first attempt at psychic functioning, after which the success rate drops sharply, to be built up again gradually through further training.

Gestalt: A structure or configuration of physical, biological, or psychological phenomena so integrated as to constitute a functional unit with properties not

derivable from its parts in summation.

Horizontal: Parallel to the plane of the horizon.

I/A/B Sequence: The core of all CRV structure, the "I/A/B" sequence is the fundamental element of Stage I. It is composed of the ideogram; the "A" component, or "feeling/motion"; and the "B" component, or first analytic response to the signal line.

Idea: Mental conception; a vague impression; a hazy perception; a model or archetype.

Ideogram: A picture, a conventionalized picture, or a symbol that symbolizes a thing or an idea but not a particular word or phrase for it. In coordinate remote viewing, the reflexive mark made on the paper as a result of the impingement of the signal on the autonomic nervous system and its subsequent transmittal through this system to the arm and hand muscles, which transfers it through the pen onto the paper. There are four types of ideograms: single, double, multiple, and composite.

Impact: A striking together; changes, moods, emotions, sometimes very gross, but may be very weak or very subtle.

Inclemencies: Personal considerations, such as illness, physical discomfort, or emotional stress, that might degrade or even preclude psychic functioning.

Intangibles: (Stage IV) Qualities of the site that are perhaps abstract or not specifically defined by tangible aspects of the site, such as purposes, non-physical qualities, categorizations, etc.; i.e., "governmental", "foreign", "medical", "church", administrative, "business", "data-processing", "museum", "library", etc.

Learning Curve: The graphic representation of the standard success-to-session ratio of a remote viewer trainee. The typical curve demonstrates high success for the first one to a few attempts, a sudden and drastic drop in success, then a gradual improvement curve until a relatively high plateau is reached.

Limen: The threshold of consciousness; the interface between the subconscious and conscious.

Liminal: At the limen, verging on consciousness.

Mass: Extent of whatever forms a body--usually matter.

Matrix: Something within which something else originates or takes form or develops. A place or point of origin or growth.

Mobility: The state or quality of being mobile.

Monitor: The individual who assists the viewer in a coordinate remote viewing session. The monitor provides the coordinate, observes the viewer to help insure he stays in proper structure (discussed below), records relevant session information, provides appropriate feedback when required, and provides objective analytic support to the viewer as necessary. The monitor plays an especially important role in training beginning viewers.

Motion: The act or process of moving.

Neuron: "A nerve cell with all its processes." The apparent fundamental physical building block of mental and nervous processes. Neurons are the basic   element

in the formation of cognitrons, and may be linked into varying configurations by the formation or rearrangement of synapse chains.

Noise: The effect of the various types of overlay, inclemencies, etc. that serves to obscure or confuse the viewer's reception and accurate decoding of the signal line.

Objectify: To cause to become or to assume the

character of an object. To externalize visually.

Objectification: The act of physically saying out loud and writing down information. In coordinate remote viewing methodology, objectification serves several important functions: recording of information derived from the signal line; re-input of information into the system as necessary for further prompting; and expelling of non-signal line derived material (inclemencies, AOLs, etc.,) that might otherwise clutter the system and mask valid signal line data.

Objects: (Stage V) A thing that can be seen or touched. "Objects" can be understood as those physical items present at the site that helped cause the cognitron to form in the viewer's mind and hence prompt his appropriate response.

Overtraining: The state reached when the individuals learning System is over-saturated and is "burned out," analogous to a muscle that has been overworked and can no longer extend or contract until it is allowed to rest and rebuild fibers that have been broken down by the stress, or reinforce those that have been newly acquired by new demands placed upon the muscle.

Peacocking: The rapid unfolding, one right after another, of a series of brilliant AOLs, each building from the one before, analogous to the unfolding of a peacock's tail.

Perceptible: That which can be grasped mentally.

Prior Emanations: Those emanations which are

responsible for the formation of cognitrons on which AOLs are based. Prior emanations, like other emanations, may be profitably decoded and objectified in Stage V.

Prompt/Prompting: To incite to move or to action; move or inspire by suggestion.

Ratcheting: The recurrence of the same AOL over and over again as if trapped in a feedback loop.

Rendering: Version; translation; drawing (often highly detailed).

Remote View: Acquire, through perception, information about a site that is at a different physical location or in a different time frame than that of the person reporting.

Remote Viewer: Often referred to in the text simply as "viewer," the remote viewer is a person who employs his mental faculties to perceive and obtain information to which he has no other access and of which he has no previous knowledge concerning persons, places, events, or objects separated from him by time, distance, or other intervening obstacles.

Remote Viewing (RV): The name of a method of psychoenergetic perception. A term coined by SRI-International and defined as "the acquisition and description, by mental means, of information blocked from ordinary perception by distance, shielding, or time."

Self-Correcting Characteristic: The tendency of

the ideogram to re-present itself if improperly or incompletely decoded.

Sense: Any of the faculties, as sight, hearing, smell, taste, or touch, by which man perceives stimuli originating from outside or inside the body.

Sensory: Of or pertaining to the senses or sensation.

Signal: A sign or means of communication used to convey information. In radio propagation theory, the modulated carrier wave that is received by the radio or radar receiving set.

Signal Line: The hypothesized train of signals emanating from the matrix and perceived by the remote viewer, which transports the information obtained through the coordinate remote viewing process.

Sketch: To draw the general outline without much detail; to describe the principle points (idea) of.

Space: Distance interval or area between or within things. "Empty distance."

Spontaneous ideogram: An ideogram that presents itself at any time in the session other than the initial Stage I I/A/B sequence. As with any ideogram, the A and B components should be decoded and objectified, followed by Stage IIs, etc.

Subconscious: Existing in the mind but not immediately available to consciousness; affecting thought, feeling, and behavior without entering awareness.   The

mental activities just below the threshold of
consciousness.

Sub-Gestalt: Each major gestalt is usually
composed of a number of smaller or lesser elements,
some of which may in and of themselves be gestalts
in their own right. A sub-gestalt, then, is one of two
or more gestalts that serve to build a greater "major"
gestalt.

Subjects: "Subject" is defined as something dealt
with in a discussion, study, etc. "Subjects" are
emanations that might serve a nominative function
in describing the site, or be abstract intangibles, or
they could be more specific terms dealing with
function, purpose, nature, activities, inhabitants, etc.,
of the site.

Subliminal: Existing or functioning outside the area
of conscious awareness; influencing thought, feeling,
or behavior in a manner unperceived by personal or
subjective consciousness; designed to influence the
mind on levels other than that of conscious
awareness and especially by presentation too brief
and/or too indistinct to be consciously perceived.

Supraliminal: Above the limen; in the realm of
conscious awareness.

Switch: The tendency of emanations in Stage V
categories to switch to emanations of a different
category due to various situations arising in Stage V.

Synapse: The interstices between neurons over

which nerve impulses must travel to carry information from the senses, organs, and muscles to the brain and back, and to conduct mental processes.

Tactile: Of, pertaining to, endowed with, or affecting the sense of touch. Perceptible to the touch; capable of being touched, tangible.

Tangibles: (Stage IV) Objects or characteristics at the site which have solid, "touchable" impact on the perceptions of the viewer, i.e., tables, chairs, tanks, liquids, trees, buildings, intense smells, noises, colors, temperatures, machinery, etc.

Topics: (Stage V) "Topics" is defined as a subject of discourse or of a treatise; a theme for discussion". Closely related to "subjects," "topics" often prove to be sub-elements of one or more of the subjects already listed, and frequently are quite specific.

(To) Track: To trace by means of vestiges, evidence, etc., to follow with a line.

Tracker: A graphic representation made on paper by a remote viewer describing the outline or contour of a site or aspect of a site, produced by a series of small dots or lines.

Unconscious: Not marked by conscious thought, sensation, or feeling.

Vertical: Perpendicular to the plane of the horizon; highest point/lowest point (i.e., height or depth).

Vision: One of the faculties of the sensorum, connected to the visual senses out of which the brain constructs an image.

Volume: A quantity; bulk; mass; or amount.

Wave: A disturbance or variation that transfers itself and energy progressively from point to point in a medium or in space in such a way that each particle or element influences the adjacent ones and that may be in the form of an elastic deformation or of a variation of level or pressure, of electric or magnetic intensity, of electric potential, or of temperature.

DOCUMENT SOURCES

[1]*Letter from I. Swann to H. E. Puthoff - 15 April 1984 - Star Gate archives - Subject: Work report. (page 31) Source: Star Gate CIA Archives.*

[2]*Co-ordinate Remote Viewing (CRV) technology 1981-1983, Three year project - Author Ingo Swann. (page 6, 8) Source: Star Gate CIA Archives.*

[3]*'Coordinate Remote Viewing Stages I-VI and Beyond' - 1985. - Author Tom McNear. (Page 9, 32) Source Star Gate CIA Archives.*

[4]*Ingo Swann letter about the DIA CRV manual - 16 April 1986 (Page 89) Source: Paul H. Smith - www.rviewer.com.*

[5]*The DIA CRV Manual & comments- Author PJ Gaenir - http://www.firedocs.com/remoteviewing/.*

[6]*The DIA CRV Manual - 1986. Authors Paul H. Smith and others. - (Page 106) Source: PJ Gaenir (www.firedocs.com).*

Daz Smith And Ingo Swann- New York, 2011

ABOUT THE EDITOR

Daz smith is a CRV trained Remote Viewer and prominent Remote Viewing researcher. Daz has participated in public and private Remote Viewing projects for many of the leaders in the field and he participates in many of the online discussions, forums and social zones in the subject of Remote Viewing. Daz also publishes a print and online Remote Viewing magazine *www.eightmartinis.com* and regular Remote Viewing news, information and resources from his large Remote Viewing website and blog *www.remoteviewed.com.*

Daz previously published a book on his past psychic experiences titled: *'Surfing the psychic internet'*. Available from *Amazon.com*.

Made in the USA
San Bernardino, CA
28 June 2013